£1·50

NATIONAL COASTWATCH

SU
COUN

NATIONAL COASTWATCH

THE NCI STORY

BRIAN FRENCH

The
History
Press

First published 2009

The History Press
The Mill, Brimscombe Port
Stroud, Gloucestershire, GL5 2QG
www.thehistorypress.co.uk

British Library Cataloguing in Publication Data.
A catalogue record for this book is available from the British Library.

ISBN 978 0 7524 4929 6

Typesetting and origination by The History Press
Printed in Great Britain

Contents

Acknowledgements

This book would not have been possible without the help of the NCI, the stations and the willing scribes who sent me written and photographic contributions. I am especially indebted to those colleagues who went the extra (nautical) mile and sent CD compilations and download sites in response to my pleas for 'more photographs'.

Many thanks to Tony King and Peter Waters for their early support, to Jon Gifford, the NCI chairman, who gave me many valuable contacts, to Mike Newbold, and to Joan Gross who filled in the large gaps in my knowledge of NCI with her supply of *Shorewatch* magazines, and to her successor Mike Smith.

To Dave Searle (HMCG Falmouth) and Alan Tarby (Cox'n RNLI Padstow) for their contributions and support.

To Amy Rigg, my very supportive editor at The History Press.

Finally, thanks to Sue, my wife, who has (more or less patiently) tolerated my umbilical attachment to the computer and proofread this document in its many stages.

I hope I have done you all justice.

Brian French
February 2009

'I am a thirty-five-year-old local sports diver, married with two children. Approximately five years ago while on an evening dive aboard a local charter boat, I found myself separated from the boat in a strong current and darkening sky. Although an experienced diver, my torches failed and I was unable to signal the boat. With my BCD fully inflated I could only watch the search, and with sea conditions worsening I was drifting very quickly up the east side of Portland. I could see the SAR helicopter close to where I had originally surfaced. Forty minutes passed and the helicopter returned to its station. After ninety minutes drifting into the 'race' off Portland Bill, and in near darkness, my dive boat finally appeared and recovered me from a very rough sea. It wasn't until I was safely back onboard that I discovered that NCI Portland had been monitoring my position all the time and sent the boat to my rescue.

It is my belief that if it had not been for NCI Portland my children would have grown up without their mother.'

Foreword

It is with much pleasure that I write these lines for the first comprehensive history of the National Coastwatch. It is a fascinating story and should be read, particularly, by all who work or enjoy the leisure of our coastline. Many will even find it surprising.

NCI has come a long way since starting in 1994. We now operate thirty-nine stations with 1,500 volunteer watchkeepers working mostly year round. Thirteen more stations are under negotiation. In 2008 we offered 173,593 hours of organised coastal surveillance, actively assisting in over 100 serious incidents along the coast, at NO cost to the public! These included all manner of situations from yachts and powerboats in distress, de-masted windsurfers, kite boarders and troubled divers to Second World War bombs on beaches and walkers injured on rocks or cut off by rising tides.

The NCI lives by public/private donations. We usually operate in remote parts of the coast, so are not well known. Our prime interest is the safety of all those along the coast within the purview of our stations, in cooperation with the search and rescue organisations concerned. Over 70 per cent of NCI stations are formally listed assets within the National SAR, coordinated by the Maritime and Coastguard Agency.

National Coastwatch will, as a charity, continue to flourish and expand with the help of our dedicated members and the generosity of the public supporting us.

On behalf of the NCI and its trustees, I wish to express sincere thanks to Brian French for compiling this book, and to all those NCI members who contributed to his worthy venture.

Jon Gifford
Chairman NCI

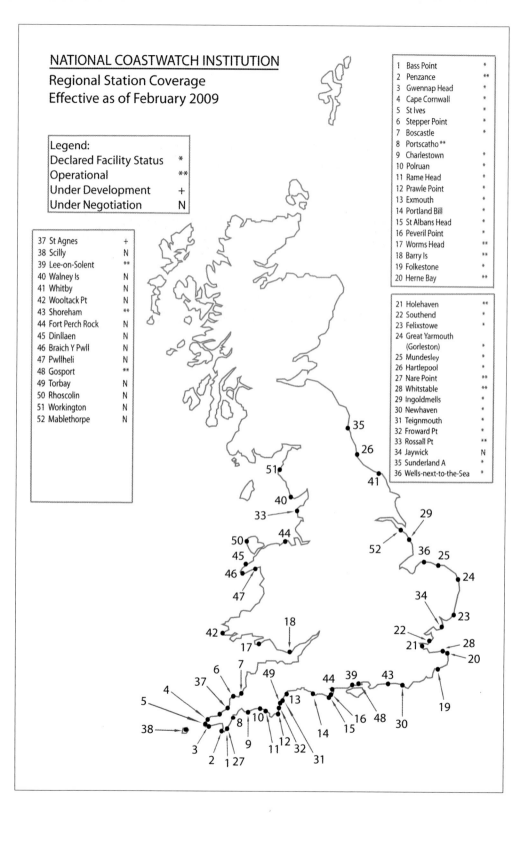

NATIONAL COASTWATCH INSTITUTION

Regional Station Coverage
Effective as of February 2009

Legend:
Declared Facility Status   *
Operational   **
Under Development   +
Under Negotiation   N

1	Bass Point	*
2	Penzance	**
3	Gwennap Head	*
4	Cape Cornwall	*
5	St Ives	*
6	Stepper Point	*
7	Boscastle	*
8	Portscatho **	
9	Charlestown	*
10	Polruan	*
11	Rame Head	*
12	Prawle Point	*
13	Exmouth	*
14	Portland Bill	*
15	St Albans Head	*
16	Peveril Point	*
17	Worms Head	**
18	Barry Is	**
19	Folkestone	*
20	Herne Bay	**

21	Holehaven	**
22	Southend	*
23	Felixstowe	*
24	Great Yarmouth (Gorleston)	*
25	Mundesley	*
26	Hartlepool	*
27	Nare Point	**
28	Whitstable	**
29	Ingoldmells	*
30	Newhaven	*
31	Teignmouth	*
32	Froward Pt	*
33	Rossall Pt	**
34	Jaywick	N
35	Sunderland A	*
36	Wells-next-the-Sea	*

37	St Agnes	+
38	Scilly	N
39	Lee-on-Solent	**
40	Walney Is	N
41	Whitby	N
42	Wooltack Pt	N
43	Shoreham	**
44	Fort Perch Rock	N
45	Dinllaen	N
46	Braich Y Pwll	N
47	Pwllheli	N
48	Gosport	**
49	Torbay	N
50	Rhoscolin	N
51	Workington	N
52	Mablethorpe	N

The History
and Development
of the NCI

Prologue

The National Coastwatch Institution was called into being on 18 December 1994, following the capsize of a Cadgwith fishing boat off Bass Point, Cornwall, some months earlier, with the loss of both its crew members. Accidents do happen at sea with unfortunate regularity, but the fact that this one took place in full view of a coastguard station and that no alarm was raised was considered a tragedy that could have been avoided. There was no alarm because the Coastguard Station had been closed down some years before, following a decision by the (now) Maritime and Coastguard Agency to cease maintaining a 'visual watch' on England's coast. So it was that Bass Point became the first NCI station to open, under the first female station manager, Lynn Briggs. The National Trust, owner of the Bass Point lookout, leased the property to the NCI for a peppercorn rent.

The 'Bass Point incident' may be taken as the trigger point for the birth of the NCI, but there are other antecedents which built up the pressure which led to this event. The rationale behind the decision to drop the coastguard's visual watch was a logical one and carried inevitable financial implications. It was considered that with the increase in the use of satellite technology and wireless telegraphy in shipping, where a 'mayday' signal could be picked up immediately and a lifeboat dispatched, it made little sense to keep a visual watch, which meant maintaining plants and a large workforce. As a consequence there would be no more need for the abundance of coastguard stations around the country.

Yet the pressure to streamline the Coastguard Service and be rid of some of the stations is nothing new. William Webb, in his definitive book *Coastguard: A history of the service*, illustrates that the coastguard was *ab initio* the servant of many masters, being required to carry out an abundance of conflicting tasks, being paid little, looked upon as a financial liability by successive governments from its inception, and not particularly valued by the populace. For example, in 1904-5, the Admiralty, then paymaster of the coastguard, under first Sea Lord Fisher, closed down thirty-five stations in an economy drive, and proposed in 1906 to close down all stations not required for Admiralty purposes. The Admiralty asked whether the patrolling of the coast as a precaution against smuggling was really necessary. Furthermore, it proposed, a small addition to the force of Customs, assisted by the local police, would enable them to dispense with the services of the coastguard completely! The Board of Customs and Excise, in alarm, proposed that they would take over the whole duty of coastal protection and relieve the Admiralty of all the work.

The advent of the First World War put a temporary halt to this wrangling. After the war the number of coastguard stations was steadily reduced. From a high point of 533 stations in 1870,

On watch.

there were 322 by 1925, when the Coastguard Act established a specialised force for coastwatch and lifesaving. Then came the first tragedy, a grim forerunner of Bass Point. In 1930 the *Islander*, sailing from Dartmouth to Falmouth, went down off Polperro with subsequent loss of life. Sir Arthur Quiller Couch, 'Q', publicly criticised the coastguard for not having a man in the lookout at Lantivet Bay. The board of inquiry was of the opinion that no blame could be attached, stating that:

> We are of the opinion that with the further development of wireless telegraph and telephone the need for visual watching should be gradually reduced. Unless a station is on an important traffic route or overlooks serious navigation danger the employment costs to the state of fulltime personnel on coast watching duties cannot be justified.

The sub-text of this statement can only be that one or two drownings here and there were acceptable to the bureaucrats. In the 1938 review, the number of stations was reduced further to 217. The coastguard service would eventually be centralised around a few major monitoring stations, and the number of coastguards in service would be reduced.

So it was that the numbers in the British Isles were reduced to nineteen 'state-of-the-art' rescue centres, the present figure, having the facility to gather data from vessels, plot their courses and request the launch of a lifeboat or auxiliary coastguards by pager phone.

MCA COASTAL LOCATIONS

ABERDEEN
4th Floor,
Marine House,
Blaikies Quay,
Aberdeen,
AB11 5PB
Tel: 01224 592334

FALMOUTH
Pendennis Point,
Castle Drive,
Falmouth,
Cornwall,
TR11 4WZ
Tel: 01326 317575

LONDON
Thames Barrier
Navigation Centre,
Unit 28,
34 Bowater Road,
London,
SE18 5TF
Tel: 0208 312 7380

STORNOWAY
Clan Macquarrie House
Battery Point
Stornoway
Isle of Lewis,
Western Isles,
HS1 2RT
Tel: 01851 702013

BELFAST
Bregenz House,
Quay Street,
Bangor,
Co Down,
BT20 5ED
Tel: 028 914 63933

FORTH
Fifeness,
Crail,
Fife,
KY10 3XN
Tel: 01333 450666

MILFORD HAVEN
Gorsewood Drive,
Hakin, Milford Haven,
Pembrokeshire,
SA73 2HB
Tel: 01646 690909

SWANSEA
Tutt Head,
Mumbles,
Swansea,
SA3 4EX
Tel: 01792 366534

BRIXHAM
Kings Quay,
Brixham,
Devon,
TQ5 9TW
Tel: 01803 882704

HOLYHEAD
Prince of Wales Road,
Holyhead,
Anglesey,
North Wales
LL65 1ET
Tel: 01407 762051

PORTLAND
Custom House Quay,
Weymouth,
Dorset,
DT4 8BE
Tel: 01305 760439

THAMES
East Terrace,
Walton on Naze,
Essex,
CO14 8PY
Tel: 01255 675518

CLYDE
Navy Buildings,
Eldon Street,
Greenock,
Strathclyde,
PA16 7QY
Tel: 01475 729988

HUMBER
Limekiln Lane,
Bridlington,
East Yorkshire,
YO15 2LX
Tel: 01262 672317

SHETLAND
The Knab,
Knab Road,
Lerwick,
Shetland,
ZE1 0AX
Tel: 01595 692976

YARMOUTH
Havenbridge House,
North Quay,
Great Yarmouth,
Norfolk,
NR30 1HZ
Tel: 01493 851338

DOVER
Langdon Battery,
Swingate,
Dover, Kent,
CT15 5NA
Tel: 01304 210008

LIVERPOOL
Hall Road West,
Crosby, Liverpool,
Merseyside,
L23 8SY
Tel: 01519 313341

SOLENT
44a Marine Parade West,
Lee-on-Solent,
Hampshire,
PO13 9NR
Tel: 023 9255 2100

In its publicity the Maritime and Coastguard Agency proudly states:

> It is no matter that you are a hundred miles along the coast from their watch room or far over the horizon. Satellite communications enable Coastguards to hear the distress calls of seafarers and coastal users who less than a hundred years ago would have hoped in vain that their feeble flares or cries might be seen or heard.

All of which is true, but it overlooks the problems of small boats either without radios or whose radios have failed, and the huge increase in water-based sports; pleasure craft, canoes, surfers and divers, not to mention paragliders and coastal walkers. These are pastimes taken up by a sometimes enthusiastic but uninformed public. Anyone can take a boat out to sea. A Board of Trade working party of the 1980s reported that pleasure craft 'incidents' had risen from 426 in 1948 to 4,811 in 1973.

A 'RARA AVIS': CAPTAIN STARLING LARK

If the above account has shown that 'logic is the process of going wrong with certainty', and that the withdrawal of the visual watch would inevitably lead to more incidents both at sea and on shore, the stage was set for a personality who was ready to seize the opportunity and make things happen. That 'rare bird' was Captain Tony Starling Lark, a North Sea pilot. He had been increasingly concerned at the number of accidents between large merchant vessels and fishing boats, particularly in the Dover Straits. Three fishing boats, the *Margaret & William II*, *Ocean Hound* and the *Wilhelmina J* had all been sunk in separate collision incidents, with heavy loss of life, in 1991. To investigate these losses Starling Lark took a BBC film crew and fishing boat skipper, himself a victim of a collision with a merchantman, on a normal pilot assignment from Brixham to the Continent on a large container vessel.

This experience illustrated to Starling Lark the different views and attitudes of the skippers of different vessels. Neither he nor the fishing boat skipper knew of each other's problems in handling their craft, the different requirements each had when using the same stretch of water and the need for them both to make a living from the sea. As a consequence of this, Starling Lark led the formation of the Sea Safety Group (SSG), which was a group of like-minded mariners interested in raising awareness of each other's problems and needs. The SSG, through its quarterly magazine, *Signal*, produced many expert papers on such items as Ro-Ro ferry safety, and the safety problems of Flags of Convenience. The magazine ran from 1990 to 2003, and one article in Lloyd's List was headed 'Ginger group'. This was one of the aims of the SSG, and it developed strong connections as a lobbying group with the Houses of Parliament.

Starling Lark's next experience led, via the Bass Point incident, to the founding of the NCI. In 1994 he was boarding a ship off Brixham in a strong easterly gale and remarked, jokingly, that if he fell overboard then at least the lookout on Berry Head would see him. He then learned the truth, that the coastguard lookout was no longer being maintained, and this, followed closely by the Bass Point drownings, led Peter Rayment, a deep sea fisherman and member of the SSG, to suggest that they try to acquire the Bass Point lookout, bring it up to working order and staff it with a volunteer 'brigade'.

So the NCI was born, in October 1994, in the Lizard football club house. From such a humble beginning further lookout stations were 'reclaimed' by various negotiation strategies. The *Western Morning News* of 27 October 1994 wrote:

> The study of Capt Tony Starling Lark is the power house for what will become a reprieve for many lookout posts and regular watches by the auxiliary Coastguards around Britain … he proposes a seven-point plan for twenty-nine watch houses to be reopened.

Starling Lark acquired funding for the rebuilding of Portland NCI from the Navigators & General, part of Eagle Star Co. Others who were very involved from the early days were Edwin Derriman, Cornwall fisheries officer, Lucille Starling Lark for organising Shorewatch membership, and Capt Anthony Ferguson who worked determinedly behind the scenes. Peter Waters, who at the time of writing is still negotiating the acquisition of yet another station, has been involved in the setting up of nine NCI stations – quite a record! As in all 'families', strong personalities do clash on occasions, and the SSG and the NCI eventually went their separate ways. The SSG still lives on in the Shorewatch stations at Sheringham, Pakefield and North Denes.

At present there are thirty-nine NCI stations and affiliates, all manned by volunteers, around the coast, with a further thirteen under negotiation. This book represents an attempt to bring information on the stations together and celebrate our development.

The Role of the Coastwatch

The National Coastwatch Institution has taken upon itself the following roles:

To maintain a visual watch along the UK coastline
To locate vessels and persons in difficulty
To keep watch over vulnerable craft and other coastal activities
To monitor Channel 16 (VHF distress frequency)
To safeguard the environment, including coastal and maritime wildlife
To monitor, record and communicate local weather conditions
To provide information to mariners, fishermen and coastal walkers
To observe and report as appropriate to the emergency services and Customs and Excise

All stations are manned by local volunteers, many of whom have an in-depth knowledge and experience of local conditions and seamanship. Watches are carried out in daylight hours on a shift system, and there is a 'buddy' system in place for night emergencies.

All stations are equipped with anemometers, radar and powerful binoculars, equipment which has been given by donors or bought with money raised in charity events.

Training and updating are, of course, essential. The potential watchkeeper is required to work through a syllabus covering navigation, communication, meteorology, safety, recognition and radar, and to complete exercises on chart work, tides, meteorology, communication and buoyage. A trainee watchkeeper will undertake at least six watches under supervision before becoming qualified and getting his/her coveted 'epaulettes'. Updating is maintained through regular training nights, courses in radio use and exercises with the local RNLI and other maritime bodies.

THE SHIFT

In a typical shift the watch monitors and logs all craft passing the watch point both inbound and outbound, and records the number of people on board. This is particularly important if, say, a small fishing boat is going out with only one person on board; a single-handed boat being more at risk in an emergency than one with two or three on board. Of course, if a boat went out with one person on board and came back with three, then there may be a case to alert the Customs and Excise officer! The second duty is to make regular sweeps of the horizon and the coast. In summer, in particular, the beaches and offshore areas are alive with people. Rocks are especially tempting for experimental scrambles, and falls are commonplace. In such an instance the coastwatch would phone their nearest centre, and a lifeboat and/or rescue helicopter would be requested. Sweeping the sea often leads to the detection of stray objects, netting, large logs or fuel cans which could be a danger to local shipping.

Much of the time is spent logging the walkers who use the coastal paths in the vicinity of the watch. Again, this log is referred to if someone is reported missing. If a person has gone past the watch point at a noted time and fails to make it to his/her destination then we know where to direct the search. Sometimes walkers are glad to come under the watch when they are caught in a sudden squall or when they have been taken ill. Generally they are very pleased to know that 'someone is watching out for them'. The weather, sea state, wind speed, direction and barometric pressure are logged at 9 a.m., noon, 3 p.m. and 6 p.m. The 9 a.m. reading, together with the state of the footpaths, is reported to the local tourist information centre and the noon reading is reported to the local rescue centre.

At the end of the day-shift the local rescue centre is informed, flags are taken down, all items to be taken in are taken in and those which need to be switched off are (usually) switched off and the watch securely locked. The thought of having omitted to do any of the latter haunts many a watchkeeper on his/her journey home.

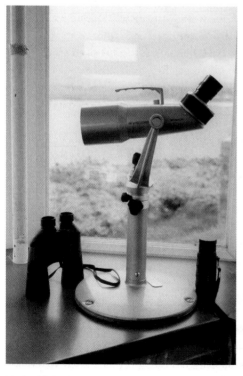

Tools of the trade.

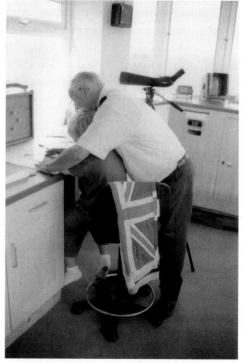

Catch 'em young.

Left: The Pelorus.

Below: Wind monitor.

EQUIPMENT AND TECHNICAL

The NCI provides a visual watch on the coast and it is often said that the chief piece of equipment we all possess is the 'mark one eyeball'. This basic tool has been augmented by binoculars and telescopes of various magnification and sophistication as stations have developed. In the early days, the bearings of vessels were made manually by using the Pelorus.

The origin of the name of this basic but still serviceable instrument is unknown, but it is thought to be the name of a scout who assisted Hannibal the Great in Italy.

The use of radar and GPS by many stations has increased their ability to plot and track vessels up to a distance of thirty-six nautical miles, even in poor visibility.

AIS (Automatic Identification Systems), used by all the main MCA stations and a few NCI watches, has made the plotting of vessels effortless. But, if the batteries fail then the Pelorus is always there.

NCI stations are also listening stations. All are equipped with radio scanners which constantly monitor the main local and national frequencies. The International Maritime Mobile (IMM) radio spectrum is divided up into sixty-plus numbered channels allocated to cover all forms of ship-to-shore and ship-to-ship communication. Channel 16 is the 'Distress, Urgency and Safety Channel', and must be kept clear at all times. Ships calling up the coastguard on this Channel are normally transferred to Channel 67, a working channel, within one minute of establishing contact. Channel O is HM Coastguard channel, used for search and rescue work and coastguard communication. Other channels to note are:

Port Operations and Harbour Authority: Channels 11, 12, 13 and 14
Intership: Channels 6, 8, 72 and 77
Marinas and Yacht Clubs: M1, M2 and Channel 80

Most stations also use a weather station which shows speed and direction of the wind. Telephone inquiries about wind conditions are frequently made by walkers and water sports enthusiasts.

An interesting variation on the Beaufort scale values was penned by one of our stations thus:

FORCE

0	Nothing moves – including watchkeepers
1	Slight draught from downstairs
2	Door closed, still get a draught
3	Paperwork flaps – but not watchkeepers
4	Pencils and pens start to roll
5	All secure, but paper work blows about
6	Side windows let in water – with sound effects
7	Windows mist up – precludes vision
8	Buckets ready
9	Windows leaking – an internal water feature is playing
10	Tower vibrates
11	No Tower
12	Phone coastguard from pub across the road

MAYDAY; PAN PAN; SECURITE; ALL STATIONS

Mayday calls, from the French *m'aide* (help me), are thankfully a rarity. It is a distress call indicating that a vessel is in grave and imminent danger, e.g. sinking or on fire. If a watchkeeper intercepts a mayday call then he is required to do... nothing! The call will generally be picked up by the local rescue station, and a rescue organised from that point. However, if no response is forthcoming from the local station then it is up to the watchkeeper to make a 'mayday relay' call to inform them that someone is in extreme difficulty. In such instances the watchkeeper can become very involved, especially if the incident is within view of his tower.

The Pan Pan call, again derived from the French *panne* (breakdown), is, simply put, a step down from a mayday call. The vessel is informing the local station that she has an urgent message to transmit concerning the safety of vessel or person. This may be a loss of power or an injured crewman but the vessel does not need urgent help and at that time can cope with the situation. This alerts the local station to the possibility of assistance and the lifeboat may be tasked to stand by.

Securite is a call made to all stations and vessels in the area informing them of some change of situation at sea. It may be a floating object in a shipping lane or the repositioning of light buoys.

All Stations is a call made by the local station to give general information, e.g. the weather forecast for the next twenty-four hours.

DECLARED FACILITY STATUS

Several NCI stations are now a 'Declared Facility'. This means that the station has been thoroughly monitored by a visiting party of NCI and coastguard officers and given the 'kite

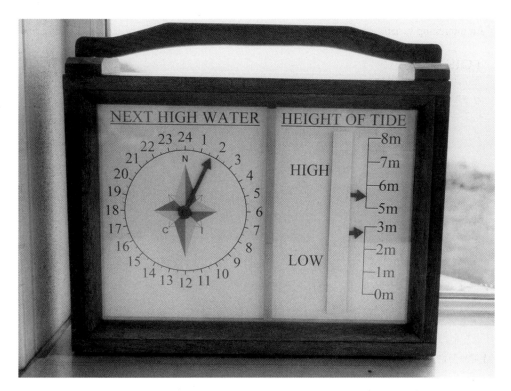

Tide indicator.

mark' of the service. All stations are encouraged to work towards Declared Facility Status (DFS). The station 'declares' to the visiting panel that is has the 'facility' to carry out the watch, and demonstrates that it has the 'status' to do so. The assessors will only examine what the station says it can do, for example a station opening at 7 a.m. will not be judged better than a station which opens at 9 a.m. The assessment process is not a test for individual watchkeepers but an overview of the whole station, its organisation, management and training. Once the assessing panel has visited the station and made its recommendation, the certificate is then issued by the chief coastguard and the station becomes a fully integrated part of the search and rescue organisation. The watchwords of the DFS inspection are, 'Spot, Plot and Report'. The watchkeepers must demonstrate that they can spot a vessel, work out its bearing from the station, and distance and if necessary, and be able to report this to their local MCA station.

Working with our Partners

HM COASTGUARD

David Searle of HM Coastguard, Falmouth:

The arrangement of coastguard Maritime Rescue Coordination Centres has evolved much over the last twenty-five years. In fact it's not all that long ago that HM Coastguard operated from tiny lookouts placed every 15 miles or so around the coast of the UK. In the 1920s, the coastguard was the eyes and ears of many organisations with coastal interests. For the Admiralty, we provided visual signalling and telegraphy and reported fleet movements. For the Board of Customs & Excise we searched vessels, supervised discharge of cargoes, collected dues and patrolled the coast. For the Board of Trade we assisted ships in distress, acted as Receiver of Wrecks and operated life-saving apparatus. We also assisted the Post Office and Lloyd's with telegraphy and wireless, and passed distress calls to the RNLI.

In 1931 an enquiry predicted that the more widespread use of radio would eliminate the need for visual watches. As technology became more sophisticated, the need for twenty-four-hour visual watchkeeping diminished. In 1951, it was recommended that visual watchkeeping should target vessels under 500 tons, as larger ships should have radio and could be monitored by a listening watch. By 1974 the UK coast was almost fully covered by the marine VHF service, operated by the Post Office, and then British Telecom, as well as HM Coastguard. As a result of this, larger coastguard stations were built to handle the majority of tasks and the increasing radio workload. We became a '999' service. Eventually the lookout stations were manned by auxiliary coastguards during daylight hours only and, finally, only during bad weather as 'casualty risk watches'.

The lookout stations were retained and could be occupied during incidents in the vicinity. But, eventually, it was decided that visual watchkeeping by HM Coastguard was no longer a requirement. Coastal observation during incidents was to be achieved from coastguard vehicles. The lookout stations closed. Coastguard watchkeeping was now carried out by technical means. We no longer carried out our original primary role of continual visual surveillance.

This paved the way for the formation of the National Coastwatch Institute. The idea was to re-open some of the coastguard lookout stations, with a view to restoring at least a daylight-

Maritime and Coastguard Agency

MCA logo.

hours visual watch. Initially, one of the coastguard lookout stations was reopened at Bass Point. Following this many lookouts were acquired for use by the NCI, and have been equipped and staffed by NCI volunteers.

The network of stations has grown and extended to the north Cornish coast and along the south coast to the east of England. From small beginnings, the NCI has grown into a significant national resource. The institute is funded entirely by voluntary contributions. This illustrates the level of respect shown by the general public towards this organisation, which is considerable.

Efforts have been made to forge operational links between HM Coastguard and the NCI. A 'memorandum of understanding' between our organisations was drafted. Liaison officers have been appointed and are actively involved in promoting awareness and cooperation between organisations. We strongly encourage all NCI staff to visit their local coastguard station, where we can demonstrate our responsibilities and capabilities. The more we understand how our organisations work, the better we will work together.

To this end, we encourage all NCI stations to achieve DFS. This sounds like a bit of a mouthful, but it is an assessment which quantifies what a particular station is capable of, and has declared it is capable of maintaining. It is useful for the coastguard to know the capabilities of the resources which we call upon. Other organisations which already hold DFS include the RNLI, Auxiliary Coastguard Service, parts of the MoD and Lloyd's of London. So it is a widespread and worthwhile achievement. Those stations which achieve DFS are permitted to use the coastguard private radio channel, and are thus more integrated into the UK search and rescue framework.

Some NCI stations are fortunate enough to have emergency response teams who will open up the station during out-of-hours periods. This can be useful especially if a lifeboat is operating within visual range, perhaps in adverse conditions. We can task the ERT in a similar manner to tasking RNLI lifeboats or coastguard rescue crews. Had the NCI tried to mimic what the coastguard had been doing, the success of the organisation may well have fallen short. It is by the very independence of the NCI that they have been able to undertake roles which HM Coastguard, by the nature of our specialised business, would not have been able to become involved with. Many diverse organisations now draw on the facilities offered by the NCI.

THE RNLI

Alan Tarby (Cox'n Padstow Lifeboat):

The seas around the coast of Britain can be very unforgiving. People often get into difficulties through no fault of their own, and, whilst our rescue services are second to none, they cannot do their job unless they know that someone is in trouble. With the ending of visual watches by HM Coastguard, areas of the coast no longer had someone watching out for those who go to sea for work or pleasure. The re-introduction of lookouts by the National Coastwatch Institution bridged this gap in the sea safety network. Now the coastguard is able to get reliable, accurate information from trained lookouts, which enable them to quickly allocate the best resources to complete the rescue.

From my perspective, as a lifeboat coxswain, it is re-assuring to know that someone is watching and listening when we go out on a rescue. Situations can change very quickly so direct communications with a coastwatch lookout are extremely useful. It must be remembered that a lookout station high on a cliff can see much further than a lifeboat operating at sea level. There are many similarities between our two organisations; we both offer a service, which is totally free to the user, the majority of our staff are unpaid volunteers and we are both funded by the generosity of the public. Naturally we feel an empathy with the members of the NCI and endeavour to support them as much as we know they support us.

Above: RNLI logo.

Right: Cox'n Tarby docks the *Spirit of Padstow*.

Reclaiming the Watch

In order for any NCI station to come on stream, a considerable amount of thinking, planning, negotiating, cajoling, fundraising, recruiting and travelling has to take place. There is also a considerable amount of frustration, annoyance and the tearing out of hair – for those NCI officials who have any hair left. Jon Gifford, chair of NCI, has no little experience in this area, and this account covers some of the questions which he has to consider when looking for a suitable venue.

a) The Site. Will a watch station at this site enhance the safety of the public in this area? Does the site have a wide purview? Is it 'busy'? This is usually ascertained by a thorough survey of local sources covering all aspects of activity. Is it a hazardous area? Is it accessible with reasonable ease (noting that there is an inverse ratio between 'watchkeeper age' and 'reasonable ease')?

A derelict Nare Point.

b) The Premises. What is the present state of the building? What facilities if any still exist? Can it be repaired? Is the owner agreeable to offering NCI a tenancy on acceptable terms, say a ten to fifteen-year lease or license? What restrictions may be put on NCI activity?

c) Staff. Is there a likely source of volunteers within a two to ten-mile radius of the site? An approximate figure of twenty-five staff is needed to open for three or four days per week, and about fifty for a full week. One or two public meetings are usually needed to answer this question as well as to outline NCI plans.

d) Funding/Local Cooperation. Visit parish/borough/district councils to introduce NCI and obtain/ascertain support for new station. Visit local societies, media and those having local influence. What grants might be available?

e) Estimated Costs. Take into account legal costs – planning and lease; renovation and new building costs, equipment costs and training costs. Also, setting up costs of travel, mileage and subsistence.

f) Final Questions. Is the project cost effective? Will donated funds be well spent?

So it doesn't happen by magic!

IS THE NCI WORTH IT?

A rather abrupt but fair question: if we have the coastguard (MCA), the RNLI, the RNAS and the local mobile coastguards ready to go into action in emergencies, then what can two (possibly elderly) watchkeepers contribute? Quite simply, the watchkeeper is in many cases the first and sometimes only person who sees the distress flare, observes the kite surfer in difficulties, or, widening his or her brief, spots the farm animal or family pet in trouble. A few recent examples will suffice:

NCI Newhaven (1 January 2008) was first responder to Kasey, a German Shepherd, who had fallen 75ft down the cliff at Newhaven Fort. Newhaven coastguard was notified and successfully retrieved the dog.

NCI Wells (July 2008) observed a family of five crossing the harbour entrance to a sand bank (Bob Hall Sands), apparently in ignorance of the siren warning that the tide was incoming. The father carried two of the four children back and towed the third over in a dinghy. The remaining child panicked as the channel deepened and the father remained with the boy. The watchkeepers notified Great Yarmouth coastguard and the lifeboat was scrambled. A successful rescue ensued.

NCI Gwennap Head (July 2008) instigated the rescue of a cow trapped on a ledge 150ft below the cliff path (see colour section, picture 4). The rescue was carried out by the combined forces of RNAS Culdrose, the coastguard cliff rescue, the fire brigade animal rescue, the RSPCA and a ministry vet!

NCI Stepper Point (17 August 2008) spotted what appeared to be a red flare issuing from a rain bank. Confirmed that there was a blue/white Rigid Inflatable Boat (RIB) at that heading, Falmouth coastguard were informed. Padstow lifeboat and rescue Helo 193 was scrambled, and the crew of one picked up. The RIB was towed to Padstow by lifeboat.

NCI Portland Bill (21 August 2008) first spotted the French yacht *Bastet* capsize in the notorious Portland Race. A successful rescue was completed by RNLI Weymouth, coastguard Helo 106, and the fishing vessel *Portland Isle*

Yacht *Bastet* waits for rescue during the Portland Race.

NCI Folkestone. An off-duty watchkeeper noticed a fully clothed woman in the sea. The watchkeeper notified the police and stayed to keep an eye on the woman until they arrived. The woman was taken to hospital.

Michael Grey of Lloyd's List has called the NCI 'a modern day national treasure'. Closer to home we have the comments of the visitors to our stations: 'a magnificent job' … 'wonderful that the station has opened again' … 'just glad that you are watching out for us'.

So yes, we are worth it!

Shorewatch

Shorewatch is a fund-raising organisation working for the National Coastwatch Institution. Subscribers pay £15 per year to become a supporter and receive copies of the *Watchkeeper* newsletter. The newsletter is sent out three times a year, in spring, summer and autumn. It contains news from all the stations around the UK coast, and is an effective fundraiser.

To become a Shorewatch supporter or to send donations please write to:

NCI 'Shorewatch'
c/o Mike Smith
Lavender Cottage, Darite
Liskeard, PL14 5JY
Email: shore.watch@virgin.net

NCI WEBSITE

You will find all the news and views of the NCI at www.nci.org, from where you can follow leads to the websites of individual stations. The website, which has recently been redesigned, is maintained by Ray Rigg. Email: ray.rigg@talktalk.net or ncipolruan@talktalk.net

NCI SHOP

All items of uniform and NCI promotional material can be had from:

Barry Milford,
Fishwicke House,
Landscore Rd, Teignmouth,
Devon, TQ14 9JU
Email: ncishop@btinternet.com

NCI Record 2007 (2008)

VESSELS IDENTIFIED AND LOGGED

Commercial/Military: 112,401 (172,424)
Pleasure: 120,560 (169,008)

    232,961 (341,432)

WATCH HOURS KEPT

Double-manned: 138,756 (162,148)
Single-manned: 34,837

    173,593

WATCHKEEPERS

Trained/Trainee: 1,588 (1,628)
Auxilliaries: 109 (103)

    1,697 (1,731)

INCIDENTS

MCA: 362 (504)
Police: 22 (90)
Ambulance: 114 (109)

    498 (703)

One incident is reported every fourteen days.
NCI initiated forty-one (fifty-two) lifeboat rescues.

Guide to
the Stations

West Cornwall Region

NCI BASS POINT

Station: Bass Point, The Lizard, Helston, Cornwall TR12 7PE
Tel: 01326 290212
Station Manager: Treve Harris 'Durgan', 12 Weeth Close, Camborne, TR14 7JJ
Tel: 01209 613997
Email: rtreveharris@aol.com
Website: www.nci-basspoint.co.uk
MCA Station: Falmouth
Declared Facility Status: 1999
Number of Volunteers: 45
Watch Hours: 08.00 – 20.00 (summer) 08.00 – 16.00 (winter)

HISTORY
The history of Bass Point, the country's first and most southerly station, is the history of the NCI (see Chapter 1).

The tragedy of losing the Cadgwith fishing boat with her two crewmen, which occurred within sight of a coastguard station which had been decommissioned only months before, inspired like-minded locals to press for the restoration of the 'visual watch', and the NCI as a body was created. Bass Point was opened by the NCI on 18 December 1994, and officially opened by actress Jenny Agutter, now an honorary member.

LOCATION
49 57.8N 005 11.15W grid SW 716119

Bass Point is situated on the Lizard peninsula and stands at 295ft above sea level (90m). It is the most southerly point in England and withstands gales in winter gusting up to Force 11. The lighthouse on Lizard Point is located on the site of the first lighthouse in Cornwall, built by Sir John Killigrew, against local opposition, in 1619. The present light has a candlepower of five-million and can be seen from twenty-one miles out. Pen Oliver, west of the lookout, was the cliff from which the Spanish Armada was first sighted in 1588.

Lloyds Signal Station.

THE WATCH: TRAFFIC AND INCIDENTS

The station monitors the sea off the Lizard, which has no traffic separation zones. Numerous merchant and commercial vessels ply the area and tend to take the shortest distance between two points, which brings them into the waters used by local fishing boats with their dan buoys and crab pots. We also have numerous yachts, powerboats and dive boats in the vicinity, and on the adjacent coastal path, in the summer months, many hundreds of walkers pass by the station. We log those whom we consider to be possibly vulnerable. Add to this rock climbers and cliff scramblers and we have a very busy station.

Lloyds of London has a monitoring station here about 100m behind the lookout. It is now privately owned and a listed building.

We log all ships passing the station within seven to eight nautical miles of the lookout. This amounts to almost 600 commercial vessels per month.

Being a watchkeeper is no fun if you can't see out of the window! Bass Point attempted to rectify this problem by installing three heavy-duty windscreen wipers facing east, south and west. This means that in the heaviest weather – rain, gales, sleet and spray – a large section of the lookout windows can be cleared so that the binoculars can focus on small objects.

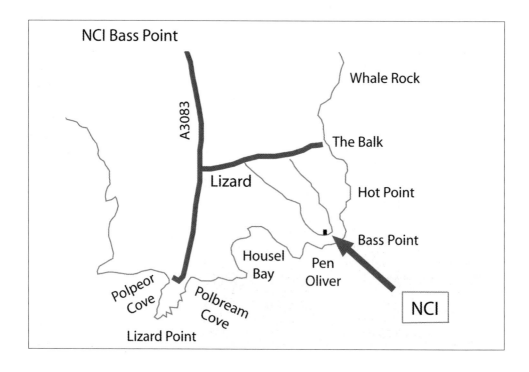

NCI CAPE CORNWALL

Station: Cape Cornwall, St Just, Cornwall
Tel: 01736 787890
Station Manager: Christine Bishop, 13 Carn Bosavern, St Just, Penzance, Cornwall, TR19 7QX
Tel: 01736 786614
Email: christineincornwall@btinternet.com
Website: www.nci.org/stations/
MCA Station: Falmouth
Number of Volunteers: 34
Watch Hours: 08.00 – 16.00 (to 20.00 in summer)

HISTORY

NCI Cape Cornwall was opened in April 1996 in the former coastguard lookout which was abandoned in the 1970s. In fact, Cape Cornwall kept going a little longer than some as it remained open, part time, as a Bad Weather Reporting Station. But it did eventually close, and remained so for over fifteen years. It had served the community well. The local fishermen, often going out twice a day on the tides in their small boats to throw lines to catch mackerel or to haul up their lobster pots, felt comforted by the fact that there was always someone up there on duty logging their movements and watching for their safe return from the little wooden lookout perched precariously on the cliff edge. Fishing was and still is very much a part of the local community in St Just and surrounding areas, and its tradition has been passed down through the generations.

In November 1995 we were deeply saddened by the loss of three male friends who tragically lost their lives whilst on a fishing trip when their vessel sank in calm seas off the coast of Brixham. Shortly after this tragic event, in February 1996, representatives of the National Coastwatch Institution came to St Just with a view to reopening the watch. They held a public meeting and asked for volunteers to help set up the station, which at that time was being used by the Cornwall Wildlife Trust as a part-time dolphin watch, a role it still retains today. The building was leased to the NCI by the National Trust. Annie Peacock, who knew many people through

her involvement in community projects, offered her services as station secretary, to initiate a working party and get the station redecorated and in working order.

The next few months proved very challenging, and it was 'all hands on deck'. The volunteers would go up there in gale force weather conditions, with no electricity, no running water, and no phone. The outside was pretty rough and it was black inside from damp and mildew – a pretty bleak prospect. However, in no time the station looked brand new again. By this time we had a team of thirty volunteer watchkeepers to cover two four-hour watches per day, seven days a week. Annie Peacock was confirmed as station controller, with Di Copperwheat as her deputy. Denis Mossman of Navigators & General, Eagle Star Insurance, officiated at the opening ceremony (performed in dense fog) and thereafter at the Cape Cornwall Golf and Country Club. There were many guests from local and district councils, seafaring and lifesaving organisations, and it was a proud day for everyone concerned.

LOCATION
50 07.6N; 005 42.56w grid sw 350318

Cape Cornwall is the only cape in England and Wales. It was so called because the map makers of the time thought that the St George's Channel and the English Channel met at this point – that being the traditional definition of a cape. They were wrong, but no one complained so we kept the name. On the cape stands the 30ft-high chimney stack which marks the site of the nineteenth-century Cape Cornwall mine.

The lookout stands on the western side of the cape, 150ft above sea level. It is made of wood and is very exposed to the prevailing south-westerlies which give raging seas and Force 12 gales in winter. On one or two occasions it has proved impossible to open the watch due to the sea breaking over the footpath below the eightieth access step (see colour section, picture 12).

The views from this lookout are staggering and encompass the whole sweep of the Atlantic from Land's End and the Longships Light (see colour section, picture 32) in the south to Pendeen watch in the north.

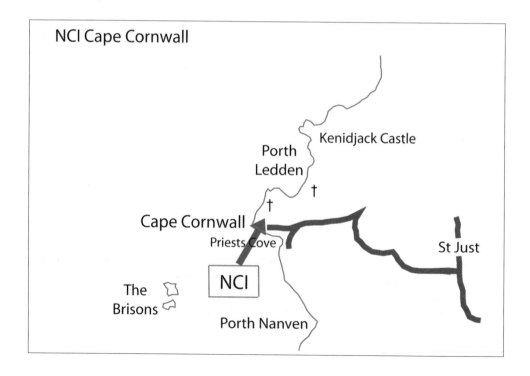

THE WATCH: TRAFFIC AND INCIDENTS

The prime job of the watch is to monitor the many cove boats, crabbers and potters which go out often with only one crew member. We are also able to monitor, both visually and by radar, the whole of the complex Land's End/Scilly Isles traffic separation scheme. We have often assisted HMCG Falmouth in monitoring vessels which have lost power or developed steering problems. We also monitor diving parties, yachts and pleasure craft, and rock climbers in the summer months, but our main preoccupation in the summer season is visiting sailors attempting to sail across the reef between the shore and the offshore rocks of the Brisons (the graveyard of many ships in the earlier days).

An incident which illustrates the vital work of NCI Cape Cornwall follows. On Thursday 26 August NCI Cape Cornwall contributed to the rescue of a fishing boat from Sennen Cove. The watchkeeper of the day writes of the experience:

> First entry in log 08.00. White open cove boat, two crew, back of Brisons – working PZ699.
>
> During the next hour or so I noticed that PZ699 had moved away and gradually disappeared into the area of the Longships lighthouse, which is 3.9 miles from Cape Cornwall.
>
> At 10.39 whilst making a general sweep with binoculars I saw what appeared to be a cylindrical upright buoy about half a mile to the back of Sharks Fin Rock. As I knew there wasn't a buoy in this position I concentrated on it and realised it was a person standing up to his knees in water and waving his arms. In fact he was standing on the submerged boat and another person was holding on to the boat, which was just below the surface.
>
> I informed Falmouth coastguard via the 999 system. They immediately alerted the Sennen Cove Lifeboat and the rescue helicopter from RNAS Culdrose. Whilst this was being carried out, the fishing vessel *Diadem* appeared and steamed from the Longships/Land's End gap towards the scene. Within a very short time they had lifted the person in the water aboard. At 10.55 the rescue helicopter was on scene and plucked the person on the submerged boat and the rescued man from the *Diadem* into the helicopter.
>
> The speed of the response to my 999 call was superb, by the coastguards, the rescue helicopter and both lifeboats from Sennen Cove.
>
> What was also remarkable about that day was to witness the strength of the tide. This had started to flood at about the time I spotted them in the water at the back of Sharks Fin Rock (10.39). When they were lifted into the helicopter their position was close to the Brisons rocks. This meant that they and their submerged boat had travelled some 2 miles in approximately 16 minutes!
>
> PZ699 was recovered by the Sennen Cove Lifeboat, towed back to Sennen and, within a short while, was recommissioned and back fishing with its crew.

AND FINALLY...

The biggest fund-raising event in July/August 2003 was the drive around the UK in a 1923 Hupmobile by Steve Unwin and his co-driver Martin Males. They visited all coastwatch stations in the UK between John O'Groats and Land's End – eleven to twelve hours driving each day at a steady 30mph – and raised £8,000, a very large sum of money for us.

NCI GWENNAP HEAD

Station: Gwennap Head, Porthgwarra, St Levan, Cornwall, TR19 9SL
Tel: 01736 871351
Station Manager: Bill Watts, 1 Godolphin Cottage, Pengersick Lane, Praa Sands, TR20 9SL
Tel: 01736 763480
Email: jobills@btopenworld.com
Website: www.nci-gwennaphead.co.uk
MCA Station: Falmouth
Declared Facility Status: March 1999
Number of Volunteers: 38
Watch Hours: 08.00 – 16.00 (to 18.00 in summer)

HISTORY

NCI Gwennap Head opened its first watch at the old coastguard station on 21 October 1996 with a handful of volunteers, a ten-minute briefing from the regional director and an old pair of Russian binoculars. Ten years later the five originals were at the tenth 'birthday' lunch, and were still going strong! While anniversaries are being celebrated, the regional coastguard station at Tol-Pedn-Penwith, to use its old name, was opened in 1906, and so, in 2006, we were remembering its centenary as well. In our ten years much has changed. New watchkeepers are properly trained rather than 'sitting by Nellie' – although in the early days Nellie was not always there, and even today two watchkeepers on watch is a luxury. Apart from Falmouth Coastguard, our mentors, we have a close relationship with the Land's End Cliff Rescue Team – now re-titled the Coastguard Rescue Service (CRS). Also, we maintain a close relationship with our sister stations from Bass Point on the Lizard, to St Ives on the north coast.

10 May 2001 was a momentous occasion for Gwennap Head because HRH the Princess Royal visited the station (see colour section, picture 13). Her helicopter flew through the Cornish mist and landed on the cliffs beside the station. Then the Princess toured the station and closely questioned the senior keepers on the range of their duties. She showed particular interest in the new radar which targeted vessels around Land's End which were not visible to the naked eye. The Royal Standard was flown from the new flagpole which, unbeknownst to HRH, had been erected the day before with many old English oaths and some very bad weather!

LOCATION
50.02.2 N 005.40.8 N grid SW 365217

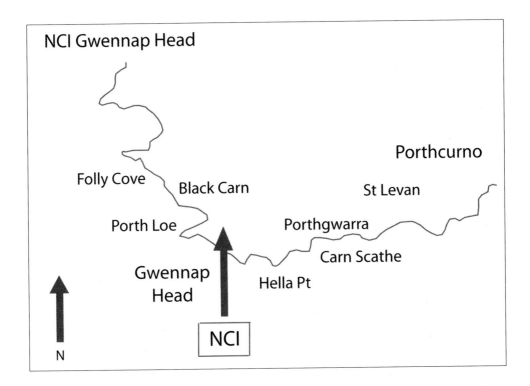

NCI Gwennap Head

Porthcurno

Folly Cove   Black Carn   St Levan

Porth Loe   Porthgwarra

                              Carn Scathe

Gwennap   Hella Pt
Head

NCI

N

Gwennap Head is located on one of the most south-westerly points of mainland Britain, and is about two and a half miles south-east of Land's End. The watch is on Tol-Pedn-Penwith point 217ft above sea level, and is owned by the St Aubyn family, headed by Lord St Levan, a patron of the NCI.

From the watch can be seen the Longships lighthouse three and a half miles away off Land's End, the Wolf Rock lighthouse seven miles south-west (notorious in past days for the long delays in relieving keepers due to bad weather), and the Seven Stones Light Vessel (off Pollard Rock where lie the remains of the Torrey Canyon of ill fame) which is moored, on 300m of chain, to the north-east of the Isles of Scilly. In good visibility (a calm, cold and clear winter's morning in December is ideal) the islands, which are twenty-eight miles off the mainland, can be seen quite clearly, including Round Island, Peninnis and the Bishop Rock lighthouses. To the east the Lizard lighthouse (the southernmost point of mainland Britain) is very clear.

In the watch's exposed position, the highest wind speed of the last century was recorded here. Extremes of weather are experienced, with the full force of Atlantic gales sometimes rising to Force 12, and the spray curling over the watch, reaching 270ft above sea level. By contrast, in calm weather sea mist/fog often prevents the watchkeeper from seeing anything except the balcony outside the watch windows.

THE WATCH: TRAFFIC AND INCIDENTS

From the watch all types of shipping using the Traffic Separation Scheme (TSS) off Land's End, and other small craft, are logged. Ships range from summer cruise ships (to the Isles of Scilly), tankers (to Milford Haven), vehicle carriers (to the Royal Portbury Dock, Bristol, and Irish

No flagging chaps!

ports on the Celtic Sea), feeder containers (to Irish ports), and general cargo ships (to Irish and west coast ports). On clear days large transatlantic shipping can be seen sailing west and diverging from our coast to use the Traffic Separation Scheme (TSS) to the south of Scilly. All types of fishing vessels from single-handed 'cove' boats to large beam trawlers and crabbers, both UK and continental, are monitored and logged. Fish factory ships are observed. In the summer months (like all NCI stations to a greater or lesser degree) very many yachts and small pleasure craft are logged. Quite a few of them are on passage to the Isles of Scilly (or 'Scilly', but <u>never</u> 'Scillies') or rounding Land's End to sail on the Celtic Sea or the Bristol Channel. Often the watch acts in a monitoring role during the Fastnet Yacht Race.

The watch has a good relationship with the Coastguard Rescue Service and, in August 2000, took part in a CRS exercise in which several keepers abseiled down the cliffs (150ft high) while the rest of the watch looked on with admiration, and a good deal of relief that they weren't the ones going down! Most incidents occur on the cliff path. This is the well-trodden South West Cliff Path stretching from Minehead in Somerset to Poole in Dorset.

A typical incident this year occurred when the watchkeeper, looking out of the western window, saw a man sprawled on the cliff path. He was injured and obviously in trouble. The keeper phoned Falmouth Coastguard (FCG) and, almost at the same time, a young woman appeared underneath the balcony seeking help. The man was her friend and she thought his ankle was broken (in this she was later proved correct). FCG called out the CRS who arrived and decided that they needed the Search and Rescue (SAR) helicopter from Culdrose. FCG called out the SAR which was overhead inside twenty minutes (which wasn't bad considering that the SAR wasn't even at Culdrose but exercising off Falmouth). The helicopter was unable to make a safe approach because of the angle of the cliff and the rocky crags projecting out of it. The CRS managed to move him further up the cliff. The SAR helicopter pilot took fifteen minutes to manoeuvre because the cliff wasn't built by nature to suit proximity to helicopters, but everyone knows how skilful and determined these pilots are, and this one was no exception. Eventually the man was lifted and flown to the Royal Cornwall Hospital, Treliske, Truro. The whole operation, from first sighting to hospital, took two hours and twenty minutes. This incident is not reported because it is unusual or worthy of exceptional comment but rather because it is a typical example of what can happen at Gwennap – and at any other NCI stations for that matter.

WILDLIFE

This heading, not surprisingly, includes walkers and birdwatchers. Out to sea, given the right weather and time of the year, one might expect to see basking sharks, dolphins and whales of various types. In the air there are fulmars, shags, cormorants, peregrine falcons and (the most elegant and skilful of all) gannets that provide precision exhibitions of low-level flying and high-speed diving.

Summer, of course, is a time for walkers and many, after parking at Porthgwarra, walk to Land's End. This, despite the distances given earlier, is about a four-mile walk, and because of the magnificent cliffs with their twists and turns and ups and downs, it usually takes rather longer than anticipated, and it is our task to advise walkers on this. Others just stay in the area of the watch and make use of the display room provided, and visitors can read about us or eat their lunch or tea in the display room or, weather permitting, outside in the sunshine. Birdwatchers are always welcome if only because they give watchkeepers advice and information on the local birdlife – not all of us are experts in this field.

That is Gwennap Head with its delights, advantages and problems. Watchkeepers, as noted earlier, have a wide variety of experience but, contrary to what some visitors believe, only a small number come from nautical backgrounds. Another feature of the watch is its isolation. Some volunteers travel thirty-five miles, and the nearest settlement is nearly five miles away.

NCI PENZANCE

Station: Chyandour, Penzance
Tel: 01736 367063
Email: nci.penzance@uwclub.net
Station Manager: Ann Altree
Email: gumma805@aol.com
Website: www.nci.org.uk
Number of Volunteers: 30
Watch Hours: Winter 08.00 – 16.00 (17.00 in the summer)

HISTORY

Penzance watch was built in 1940 as a searchlight tower, having a generator and a carbon arc searchlight. It supported two pieces of artillery guarding the seaward approach. At the end of the war it was used by many organisations, for multiple purposes, including the coastguard, navy, air force and, finally, the NCI. When it was leased to the NCI from the Ministry of Defence it was a very wet shell with four solid walls. In eight weeks our team of volunteers had installed new floors and all the electrics ready for the grand opening in 2002. Watch training was helped by having knowledgeable officers holding master certificates and RYS qualifications, as well as a couple of local fishermen.

By 2007 the tower was in need of further repairs to the roof and windows and, supported by Lottery funding, was reopened 'as new' in July 2008.

LOCATION

50 07.45N; 005 31.72W grid SW478309

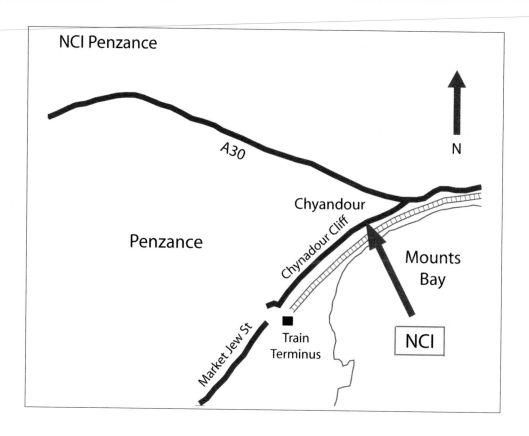

NCI Penzance

The watch tower is situated on Chyandour Cliff 65ft above sea level with a clear view over Mount's Bay. St Michael's Mount lies three miles away to the east, and Penlee Point to the south (see colour section, picture 14, of St Michael's Mount).

The *Scillonian*.

THE WATCH: TRAFFIC AND INCIDENTS

The watch monitors all traffic into Penzance and the busy fishing port of Newlyn. From Penzance the *Scillonian* ferry plies regularly between the mainland and the Isles of Scilly. There are many visiting vessels in the bay from cruise ships to dive boats and canoes. The beaches are used for all manner of water-based activities including wind and kite surfing and zap cats, not to mention the walkers on the coastal path. The following are brief examples of logged incidents which give an illustration of the work of the watch.

05.01.06	Person cut off by tide. CG team attended
05.01.06	Auxiliary CG in station assists in search for missing person
10 01.06	Monitored and reported surfer in rough sea
27.01.06	Reported MFV in difficulties – ILB attended
02.02.06	Reported red flare from yacht – ILB (Inshore Life Boat) attended
11.02.06	Yacht drifting inshore – CG and ILB attended

NCI ST IVES

Station: The Lookout, The Island, St Ives
Tel: 01736 799398
Station Manager: Keith Hodge, 3 Polwithen Drive, Carbis Bay, St Ives, TR26 2SN
Tel: 01736 797273.
Email: keiththodge@tesco.net
Website: www.nci.org.uk
MCA Station: Falmouth
Declared Facility Status: 2001
Number of Volunteers: 40
Watch Hours: 07.00 – 18.00 (summer), 07.00 – 21.00 (August), 07.00 – 16.00 (winter)

HISTORY

NCI St Ives stands on the north coast of Cornwall, on the Penwith peninsula. It is housed in the former coastguard station which is situated on the site of the old Lamprock Battery which played such a vital part in shore defence during the Napoleonic Wars. The battery was armed with six eighteen-pound cannon and six twelve-pound cannon and was manned by the Volunteer Artillery Company, formed in 1801. The remains of a gun emplacement stand to the rear of the watch house. The battery was dismantled in 1815. The name Lamprock is reputed to have been adopted by locals who used to hang a lamp on St Ives Head to guide incoming vessels to the harbour.

To the west of the NCI lookout is the chapel of St Nicholas. St Nicholas is not only the patron saint of children but also of sailors, and it is natural to assume that the latter is the reason for the dedication of this little chapel, standing as it does on the top of the island, surrounded by

sea on three sides. Unfortunately we do not know when it was originally built, though we do know that it has withstood patching and alterations since the latter half of the fifteenth century, if not earlier. Indeed, one would assume that our Cornish ancestors duly worshipped in the St Nicholas chapel before the church of St Ives was erected in 1434, although it must be remembered that the people of St Ives were forced to pray in the church at Lelant before the existing parish church was built.

St Nicholas chapel.

The town authorities have always been responsible for its upkeep. In the borough records for 1592 we find 'paid to John Kalamey for mending Saint Nicholas Chappell, is 1s 4d' and in 1538 a traveller to this part of Cornwall is recorded as saying 'There is now at the point of Pendinas a chapel of St Nicholas and a pharos for lighte for shippes sailing by night in these quarters'. Not only has this chapel served as a place of worship but it became transformed into a lookout for revenue officers in the eighteenth century, and eventually passed into the hands of the War Office who used it as a store until 1904 when the department began to pull it down, amidst local outcries. Fortunately the desecration was arrested and in 1911 Sir Edward Hain (the St Ives ship owner) restored the building to commemorate the Coronation of King George V. The chapel was restored again in 1971 through the generosity of Mr J.F. Holman with the co-operation of the then borough council. Local artists have contributed to the work, and Archimandite Barnabas of St Elias Monastery, Willand, near Cullompton, Devon, gave the *Icon of St Nicholas*.

The local churches have agreed to share responsibility for the spiritual care of the chapel, and on the 'highest point' we shall soon be seeing a visible reminder both of 'that unity which we seek and that which we already have'.

The station was first staffed on 10 August 1999, the day before the total eclipse of the sun. At that time nobody possessed a uniform and the three volunteers who manned the first watch had one pair of binoculars between them. These were on loan from the regional manager, Kevin Samson, who became the first manager of St Ives watch station. Normal watches begin at 7.00 a.m. when, in the winter months, it is still dark. Special regular exercises are carried out for volunteers operating during hours of darkness. St Ives also provides an early response facility through two teams available to man the station during 'silent hours' when the lookout is normally closed. In 2001 the station was awarded the coveted Declared Facility Status. This is still the record time for a station to be awarded DFS from its starting date.

In August 2001 the St Ives station took part in 'The Lighthouses and Lightships on Air', a two-day radio weekend. A total of 130 stations were worked, covering the whole of Europe, Russia, Canada and the USA, and the St Ives number E144 was much in demand.

LOCATION
50.13.11N; 005 28.58W grid SW 522412

The lookout commands a magnificent field of vision; the open ocean to the north and west, the beaches and the harbour, with Smeaton's wall, to the south-east, and the Godrevy Light to the north-east (see colour section).

The Godrevy Light guards the Stones, a reef lying about one and a half miles from the mainland. In December 1854 the Stones had wrecked the *Nile* with the loss of all hands. After much debate as to the site of the lighthouse, it came into operation in 1859. The light, now automatic, has a range of twelve miles. The tower is 86ft high, and is featured in Virginia Woolf's famous novel *To the Lighthouse*.

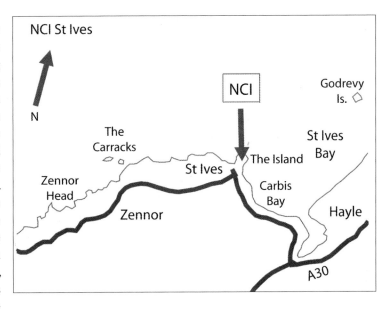

THE WATCH: TRAFFIC AND INCIDENTS

St Ives is a working port as well as one of Cornwall's premier holiday resorts, thus the watch is responsible for monitoring a variety of potentially vulnerable craft and people. These can range from trawlers and crabbers to open boats, fishermen, boardsailers, divers and swimmers, inflatable boats and lilos, as well as walkers, in the vicinity of the watch. All craft are monitored for potential breakdown, gear failure, leaks in vessels and exhausted crews.

On 29 October 2000 at 14.23 the 12,000-ton general cargo/heavy lift Egyptian vessel *Green Glory* was observed at anchor in the bay. Watchkeepers Caldwell and Ross decided to put a radar guard on her in case she moved. Within fifteen minutes of this she started to drag her anchor. St Ives contacted MCA Falmouth immediately and flashed 'U', which signifies 'You are standing into danger'. MCA Falmouth contacted *Green Glory* by VHF to inform her of this. Monitoring her over an hour by radar and 'visual', the vessel was observed to be drifting close to Carrick Rocks. Again 'U' was flashed, and she went hard astern and dropped anchor. The anchor was seen to be holding safely at 16.25. During this time NCI St Ives and MCA Falmouth were in constant conversation as to the state of the vessel. This was an excellent example of the cooperation between the NCI and the coastguard to ensure vessel safety.

One memento of the dangers of north Cornwall's coast is the remains of the boiler of the *Alba*, visible at low tide on Porthmeor Beach, which was wrecked in 1938. Could the NCI have been of service then?

Wreck of the *Alba*.

AND FINALLY...

St Ives has its own standard duly dedicated in the parish church. This is paraded on Mayor's Sunday, and is supported by the Remembrance Parade. We consider that if you support your town and the council, they will in turn support you. This has proved to be very true of St Ives.

NCI NARE POINT

Station: The Lizard, Helston, Cornwall
Tel: 01326 231113
Email: narepointnci@tiscali.co.uk
Station Manager: Alan Edwards, Treglohan Minor,
Dean Pt, St Keverne Helston, TR12 6NY
Tel: 01326 251113
MCA Station: Falmouth
Watch Hours: Summer, Friday to Monday, 08.00 – 20.00
Winter, Friday to Monday, 08.00 – 16.00

HISTORY

A former Cold War naval tracking station at Nare Point, near Manacaan, one of only two such structures still remaining in Cornwall; this building has been converted into a lookout station for the NCI. Monies have been raised for the renovation by the National Trust Enterprise Neptune Campaign, the MoD Veterans Challenge Fund and the Tanner Trust. From Nare Point, thanks to the installation of a new window in the north side of the building, the watch has 290 degrees of vision, taking in Gillan harbour, the mouth of the Helford River, Maenporth Bay, Falmouth's southern beaches, St Anthony's Head Light, and the whole of the bay south to the Manacles.

LOCATION
50 05.12N; 005 04.6W grid sw800251

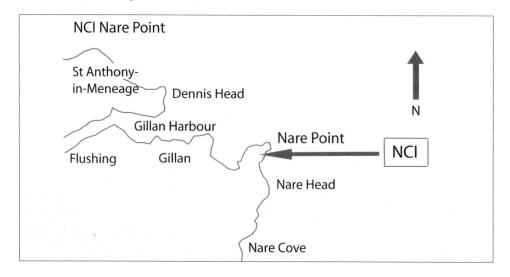

North and East Cornwall Region

NCI BOSCASTLE

Station: Old Coastguard Lookout, Boscastle
Tel: 01840 25096
Email: info@nci-boscastle.co.uk
Station Manager: John Davis, Wyneglos, Forrabury, Boscastle, PL35 0DJ
Tel: 01840250741
Email: john@jgdavis.co.uk
Website: www.nci-boscastle.co.uk
MCA Station: Falmouth
Declared Facility Status: 2005
Number of Volunteers: 45
Watch Hours: 08.00 - 16.00

HISTORY

Boscastle NCI was opened by local MP Paul Tyler in June 2003. The site, in the former coastguard lookout, is one of the most distinctive of the NCI stations. It was originally built as a summer house in the early 1800s by Thomas Avery but was later leased to HM Coastguard as a lookout for the apprehension of smugglers. Its use as a coastguard station ceased in the 1970s, when it was maintained by the National Trust until the NCI took it over in 2002. The building was completely renovated by NCI volunteers who raised money with traditional sales and 'tin rattling'. Central NCI loaned £500, and two grants came from the National Lottery. Preparatory work involved a new floor, linings to walls and wiring, and installation of equipment needed for keeping watch.

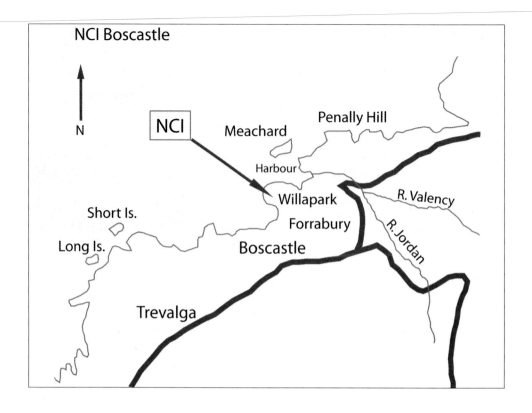

LOCATION
50 41.37N; 004 42.19W grid sx 091913

The lookout, at Willa Park, stands at a height of 320ft on the headland overlooking the harbour whose inner jetty was rebuilt in 1584 by Sir Richard Grenville, captain of the *Revenge*. The outer breakwater, destroyed by a sea mine in 1941, was rebuilt in 1962 by the National Trust. The seaward view from the lookout is spectacular, sweeping the open Atlantic from Hartland Point in the north-east to Tintagel Head in the south-west. Thirty-four miles out to sea, Lundy Island is visible on a good day.

THE WATCH: TRAFFIC AND INCIDENTS
In winter our main traffic includes passing oil tankers, cargo vessels, bulk carriers and car carriers. In summer the traffic is augmented by numerous fishing boats, yachts and pleasure craft. As the station is directly on the south-west coastal path we have a considerable number of walkers passing the lookout going to/from Boscastle to Tintagel and Crackington Haven. Recently a walker suffered a heart attack and we were able to help, through the Falmouth Coastguard, in directing the air ambulance to the nearest safe landing place from which to recover the walker. Boscastle does not have its own lifeboat, but we work closely with RNLI Bude and Padstow. We keep a safety watch on the Boscastle Gig, which has no VHF contact. As well as a human watch we keep an eye on local livestock which can wander onto the cliffs and find themselves in danger.

NCI CHARLESTOWN

Station: Landrion Point, Sea Rd, Carlyon Bay, St Austell
Tel: 01726 817068
Station Manager: Gerry Stockwell, 47 Chatsworth Way,
  Carlyon Bay, St Austell
Tel: 01726 812497
Email: gerrystockwell@fsmail.net
Website: www.nci.org.uk/stations
MCA Station: Brixham
Declared Facility Status: December 2007
Number of Volunteers: 32
Watch Hours: 08.00 - 20.00 (summer) 09.00 - 16.00 (winter)

HISTORY

There has been a lookout at Charlestown since 1928, an old photograph of that date shows it clearly marked. But in order for the lookout to be used by the NCI it had first to be 'rediscovered'. In February 2001, Peter Waters, the first station manager, identified the lookout by its roof which was just visible in the dense undergrowth. Restormel Borough Council arranged for a pathway to be cut to the lookout so that the work of clearing away the vegetation could begin. The first lease on the property was signed in September 2001. The building was in a dilapidated state, the floor and steps to the upper floor having collapsed. The doors were rotten and all the window panes had disappeared. To enable clearance work to be done, Pat Harris of Lostwithiel provided the heavy plant and arranged for 17 tons of aggregate to be delivered by Jack Kingdom of Lanivet – all at no cost. A group of students from St Austell College fitted new floors and doors as part of a training project and Imrys supplied the new stairway. In the midst of all this debris it was amazing to discover that the telephone line was still connected and the station was up and running by April 2003. It was officially opened by patron E.V. Thompson on 11 October 2003 with a blessing by Father John.

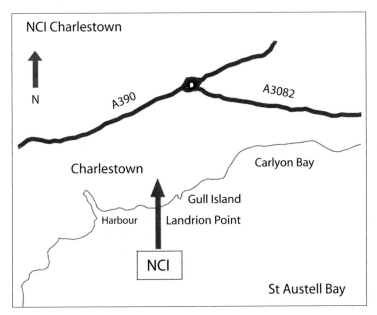

LOCATION
50 19.93N;004 44.80w
grid sx046516

The lookout commands a view of the whole of St Austell Bay with its two harbours. The bay is enclosed by Blackhead in the west and the Gribben, with its distinctive red and white daymark, in the east. Charlestown is well known for its harbour, its museum and three square riggers which have featured in many films and TV productions (see colour section, picture 5).

THE WATCH: TRAFFIC AND INCIDENTS

During the summer months the bay is busy with all types of leisure craft. Porthpean Sailing Club holds regular race days and often hosts international class dinghy races. Fishing boats from Mevagissey, Fowey and Charlestown are active in the bay all year round. Several dive boats also frequent the area in summer.

June/July 2006 saw an influx of basking sharks in the bay, and the lookout became a popular spot for viewing them.

NCI POLRUAN

Station: The Pilots Lookout, St Saviours Hill, Polruan
Tel: 01726 870291
Station Manager: John Adams, The Eyrie, Townsend, Polruan PL23 1QH
Tel: 01726 870381
Email: ncipolruan@talktalk.net
Website: www.polruan-nci.org.uk
MCA Station: Brixham
Declared Facility Status: 2001 re-awarded 2005
Number of Volunteers: 35
Watch Hours: 08.00 – 20.00 (summer) 08.00 – 16.00 (or sunset)

HISTORY

The lookout stands adjacent to the remains of St Saviour's chapel, built in the eighth century and used as a daymark by sailors throughout the centuries. The first documented evidence of this chapel was given by Robert de Boyton to the Priory of St John at Bridgewater. After 1572 it fell into disrepair, and all that remains now is a stone buttress. The lookout is at the highest point of the village, 230ft

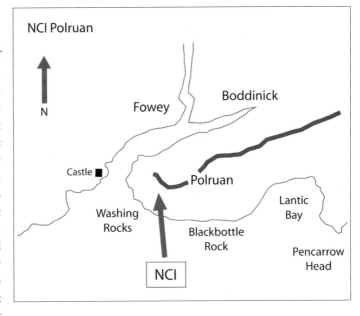

above sea level, and overlooks Fowey Harbour to the north and covers a sea watch from the Eddystone lighthouse, sixteen and three-quarter miles eastward, to the Lizard Peninsula in the south-west, Gribbin Head and the approaches to St Austell Bay in the west. The horizon is about twenty-six miles away. It was constructed in the mid-nineteenth century as a coastguard station, and was later used as the Fowey pilots' lookout. More recently it was complemented by a smaller lookout on the 'peak' which could observe vessels coming from the east close in to the shore – a blind spot for the lookout. Unfortunately this was demolished by the National Trust shortly before the NCI was established locally.

The building, rented from the Polruan Town Trust, was opened as an NCI station in April 1998 by Pete Goss, the 'round the world' yachtsman. Much of the refurbishing of the lookout was done by members' voluntary efforts, and initial fund-raising concentrated on acquiring equipment such as the anemometer and radio scanner. Polruan is proud of its 'watchkeeper's desk', custom designed and built by Ray Rigg in 2001 for a course he was attending on furniture design. The desk, installed in 2002, is designed so that all necessary equipment and information is immediately to hand.

In 2006, in cooperation with the Fowey Harbour commissioners, it was agreed that NCI Polruan would reinstate the hoisting of a 'storm cone' to give warning of gale force winds. It is thought that Fowey is one of the few ports maintaining this traditional service. Storm cones were introduced by Admiral Fitzroy in 1861. The cone is hoisted whenever a gale is forecast and indicates whether it is northerly (point up) or southerly (point down). With the advent of weather information the cone was phased out. However, vessels without a radio receiver have little warning of a Force 8 coming their way, and shoremen find that a visual check of conditions is very useful – a further example of the NCI's mandate to keep a visual watch.

The lookout is on the Cornish section of the south-west coastal path, and all walkers are logged and monitored. A lookout for marine animals and other wildlife is maintained, and all sightings are reported to sea watch.

LOCATION
50 19.58N; 004 38.05W grid SX125508

The station can be reached from Fowey by the foot ferry which operates throughout the year. On arriving at Polruan, pass the general store on your left and keep on till you reach School Lane, a footpath on your right. Follow the lane until you reach the village hall on the right, and then turn left up the footpath on the Bound (a grassy knoll). At the top of the knoll cross the road and ascend the footpath between the public toilets and the entrance to the car park. The lookout is the white building at the top.

By car, visitors should turn off the Lanteglos highway by a red telephone box at the western end of the village, where Polruan is signposted. It is about two miles to Polruan, and on arrival drive down the hill into the village and turn left into St Saviours Hill (opposite a bus stop on the right) and follow the road to the car park.

From its position the station commands superb views, and from the lookout the following maritime landmarks and places of note can be seen:

St Catherine's Castle built *c.*1542. In 1786 it housed six cannon and maintained a small garrison of Sea Fencibles, forerunners of the coastguard. It was last garrisoned during the Second World War.

Lifeboat Station established in 1922. It has an inshore RIB (No.464) and a trent-class all-weather boat *The Maurice and Joyce Hardy* (No.14).

Gribbin Head an 84ft-high daymark erected in 1832 by Trinity House on land donated by the Rashleigh family.

THE WATCH: TRAFFIC AND INCIDENTS
Fowey is a natural deepwater harbour managed as a trust port by the Fowey Harbour Commissioners. A minimum depth of 6.5m below chart datum is maintained by dredging. The port can handle ships of 17,000 dead weight tonnage, and up to 163m in length can be handled. All vessels in excess of 37.5m must have compulsory pilotage. FHC handles all the pilotage for Fowey, Par and Charlestown harbours. A speed limit of six knots applies to all craft within the harbour, which extends from St Catherine's Castle to the high watermark at Lostwithiel Bridge.

The traffic monitored by NCI Polruan is something in the region of 650 cargo vessels per year exporting china clay, 7,200 visiting yachts and six visiting cruise liners. The largest vessel brought into the harbour was the *Crystal Harmony* (now renamed *Asuka II*), weighing in at 48,000 tons. In addition, there are frequent visits from Royal Navy craft, Customs and Excise and Fisheries Protection vessels. There are up to 1,500 resident craft moored in the estuary.

AND FINALLY...
On 3 August 2003 we were proud to welcome home one of our members, Dr Kenneth Gibson, who became the fourth oldest man to cross the Atlantic single-handed. Deputy Manager Colin Merrill made two trips out to the Dodman, with Kenneth's wife and family, aboard the *Black Morwenna*, and finally met up with the *Siliwen* at 7.30 a.m. A tremendous achievement!

NCI PORTSCATHO

Station: Pednvadan Point, Portscatho
Tel: 01872 580180
Station Manager: Peter Clements, Lydden, Springfield Close,
   Polgooth, St Austell, PL26 7BB
Tel: 01726 75255
Email: petershielaclem@hotmail.com
Website: www.nci.ork.uk/stations
MCA Station: Falmouth
Number of Volunteers: 15
Watch Hours: March – October and Bank Holidays.
   Three days per week 10.00 – 17.30

HISTORY
NCI Portscatho is housed in the old coastguard lookout on Pednvadan Point in south Cornwall.
Built in the 1920s, this is a very basic lookout, and possibly the smallest NCI station in existence
(see colour section, picture 2). The stone structure is hexagonal in shape with the windows
on the seaward (east) side. It can accommodate two (slim) watchkeepers. Like many of these
remote lookouts there is no water, electricity or ablutions. There is a half-mile walk to the
lookout from the village of Rosevine, so our volunteers here are a very dedicated body.

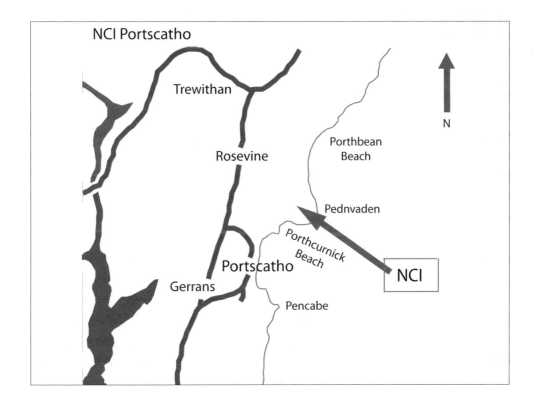

LOCATION

50 11.1N; 004 58.1W grid sw882360

The lookout takes in the sweep of Gerrans
Bay. In the immediate vicinity are the beaches
of Porthchurch, Porthbean and Pendower.
The eastern view takes in Nare Head and
Gull Rock as well as the notorious Dodman
Point beyond with its granite cross erected
in 1898 and dedicated to shipwrecked souls.
    To the south is Portscatho Harbour itself.

Dodman Cross.

NCI RAME HEAD

Station: Old Coastguard Lookout, Rame Head, Cawsand, PL10 1LH
Tel: 01752 823706
Email: info@nci-ramehead.org.uk
Station Manager: Peter Creber, Moorland Ways, Whistley Down, Yelverton, Devon, PL20 6EN
Tel: 01822 854548
Email: peter.creber@netbreeze.co.uk
Website: www.nci-ramehead.org.uk
MCA Station: Brixham
Declared Facility Status: Awarded 2004
Number of Volunteers: 56
Watch Hours: 09.00 – 19.00 (summer) 09.00 – 17.00 (winter)

HISTORY

Rame Head, with its stairway and gallery, has a long history of being a nautical lookout. First it
was a chapel, dedicated to St Michael, built in the eleventh century, and a license to worship in
it was granted in 1397. It has also served as a hermitage and a watch house. Records dated 1488
show payments made to the watchmen of Plymouth Corporation for news of approaching
vessels. In 1588 the beacon blazed as the Armada fleet was first sighted a few miles offshore.
The chapel subsequently became a huer's lookout for the arrival of the herring shoals. The
lookout is inland from the chapel. It was a Lloyds signal and reporting station in the eighteenth
century, but its service as a coastguard station was finally abandoned in 1992 when permanent
coastguard cover was withdrawn during the national reorganisation of the service.

In February 1998 several local people
met at the nearby village of Cawsand
with the idea of reopening the station
as a visual watch under the auspices of
the NCI. The Mount Edgcumbe estate
provided the building free of charge,
and naval recruits from HMS *Raleigh*,

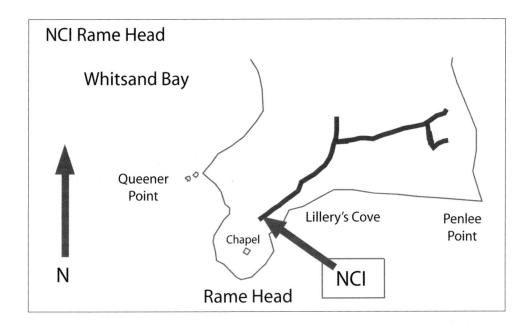

NCI Rame Head

Whitsand Bay

N

Queener Point

Lillery's Cove

Penlee Point

Chapel

NCI

Rame Head

Torpoint, renovated and painted the inside of the building. The watch was opened on 2 May 1998, with its official opening on 2 May 1999. The equipment then amounted to a log book and a pair of binoculars – the absolute bare essentials.

THE LOCATION
50 19.03N; 004 13.19W grid SX421487

The station overlooks the Rame Peninsula and, standing at an elevation of 102m, has a commanding view with a clear visibility to the south of twenty-two nautical miles. Eastwards is Bolt Head (seventeen nautical miles) and to the west Dodman Point (twenty-three nautical miles). On a very clear day the dishes at Goonhilly Earth satellite station on the Lizard are just visible forty-four nautical miles away.

Perhaps the most notable landmark here is the Eddystone lighthouse which is easily visible from the station at just under eight and a half nautical miles due south. The lighthouse, the fifth to be built, stands on the Eddystone Rocks, a notorious reef. It was to 'rid ships of this menace' that Henry Winstanley, a merchant, had the first lighthouse built, a wooden structure completed in 1698, virtually rebuilt a year later and completely destroyed by a storm in 1703, while Winstanley himself was staying there.

Jon Rudyerd built the next tower and charged a toll to passing ships. It was completed in 1708 with a tapering tower and a ship's mast up the middle to give it flexibility. It lasted forty-seven years until it was burned down by the very candles used for the light, which set fire to the roof. John Smeaton's tower, built with dovetailed granite blocks, was completed in 1759 and stood for 127 years until cracks in the cave below it were observed. In 1881 the tower was dismantled and re-erected on Plymouth Hoe where it stands today. The remains of the base of Smeaton's Tower can be seen at the side of the present lighthouse.

The present tower, designed by James Douglass, was completed in 1882 and stands at 72m high. Its original oil-powered lamps were replaced first by electric and then by solar-powered lamps. It has a helicopter deck, added in 1980, and was automated in 1982, giving two white flashes every ten seconds over a range of twenty-four nautical miles. The fog signal blasts three times every sixty seconds.

THE WATCH: TRAFFIC AND INCIDENTS

HMS *Scylla* scuttled.

The main traffic consists of vessels arriving and leaving Port Plymouth and Devonport Naval Base. Naval vessels, merchant men and fishing craft keep the lookout busy in the winter months.

Additionally, in summer there are also leisure craft, jet skis, canoes and dinghies. Many well-known sailing events are monitored, including the Fasnet Race. Warships from most NATO and other European nations take part in exercises under control of Flag Officer Sea Training (FOST). These exercises include aircraft, and test the ability of all warship systems prior to deployment.

On 2 February 2002, the timber carrier *Kodima* went aground in sight of the lookout in Whitsand Bay, shedding its cargo of cut timber. Many garden sheds or similar were constructed during this period. The vessel was eventually refloated and towed to Falmouth.

In March 2004 the first artificial reef in Europe was created by the sinking of HMS *Scylla*.

Her position can be seen from the lookout, marked by a line of buoys. On behalf of the Marine Aquarium, Plymouth, all dive boats visiting the reef are logged by the watch.

There have been concerns about the dumping of waste from the nearby docks and Tamar estuary into the sea just south-west of Rame Head. By plotting these vessels we can assure the public that waste is only dumped in the area designated, and inform the relevant agency if we suspect any contravention.

Many walkers join and leave the coastal footpath, which runs some 100m below the lookout. A large free car park ensures many visitors linger and admire the scenery in the area.

Rame Head is designated as an area of outstanding beauty. The once rare peregrine falcon can now be seen near the lookout together with cirl buntings, stonechats and linnets. Rame is a prime area for butterflies such as the clouded yellow the red admiral and, occasionally, the monarch. The light at the entrance to the station is a great attractant for moths, some of which stay on the walls of the station. The beautiful gothic, now found only on the south coast of Cornwall, Devon and Dorset, has been found several times at this station. From November to May, you will see several Dartmoor ponies grazing around our station (see colour section, picture 9).

AND FINALLY...

One amusing and touching event occurred recently whereby a grand old lady entered the lookout, put a donation in the collection box and said, 'Thank you for looking after my husband'.

The watchkeeper was rather concerned, and asked, 'Does he pass here?'

'No,' was the reply, 'His ashes are out there'.'

NCI STEPPER POINT

Station: Stepper Point, Padstow, Cornwall
Tel: 07810 898041
Station Manager: Colin Davey, 4 St Petrocs Close, Padstow, PL28 8SP
Tel: 01841 533047
Email: jucol4davey@waitrose.com
MCA Station: Falmouth
Website: www.stepper-point.co.uk
Declared Facility Status: 2006
Number of Volunteers: 50
Watch Hours: 09.00 - 18.00 (summer) 09.00 - 16.00 or sunset (winter)

HISTORY

Stepper Point stands high on the north coast of Cornwall. Along with Pentire Point opposite, it guards the entrance to the Camel estuary and the port of Padstow. The lookout commands a spectacular view north to the open sea and Lundy Island thirty-six nautical miles away and visible with binoculars on a clear day, west to Trevose lighthouse and the new lifeboat station, taking in the full sweep of the river down to Padstow in the south, and the beaches of Rock, Daymer Bay and

Polzeath to the east. At low water the sand of the 'Doom Bar', destroyer of many ships and crew over the centuries, is visible below Stepper and the quarry. The rocks of Greenaway can still prove hazardous to gale-blown vessels (see colour section, picture 8).

The lookout, 75m above sea level, was formerly the coastguard station in which the first station manager, Derek Lindsey, served his time as an aux-in-charge. It was abandoned during the MCA reorganisation in the 1980s, and in March 2000, when the NCI leased the land from the Prideaux-Brune estate, the building was a weather-beaten shell. Volunteers were recruited and work was set on to restore the station. In March 2002 the station was operational and proud of the unique feature that it was the only 'totally green' station, deriving all its power from wind and solar energy – the cost of a land line connection was and still is exorbitant! Further massive fund-raising efforts meant that by 2005 plans to expand the lookout, giving it almost 360 degrees of vision (and more room for expanding watchkeepers!) could be realised. The 'new' building was up and running by spring 2006.

LOCATION
50 34.7N; 004 56.9W grid SW913784

The lookout is accessed by foot from the north Cornwall coastal path – only fit watchkeepers survive here! From Padstow take the B3276 to Newquay. At the 'give way' sign take a very sharp right down the narrow track to Crugmeer. Follow that winding road for about two miles and, with Trelissick Farm on your right, park at the side of the road near the gate to the coast path. On foot, follow the gravel road round the field, and at the gate take the left fork up the hill. You will see the daymark tower further on your left. Keep to the right-hand path and soon you will see the lookout. The daymark, a 40ft tower built for ships to identify the entrance to the harbour in 1826, at a cost of £29, is the best guide to the lookout (see colour section, picture 1).

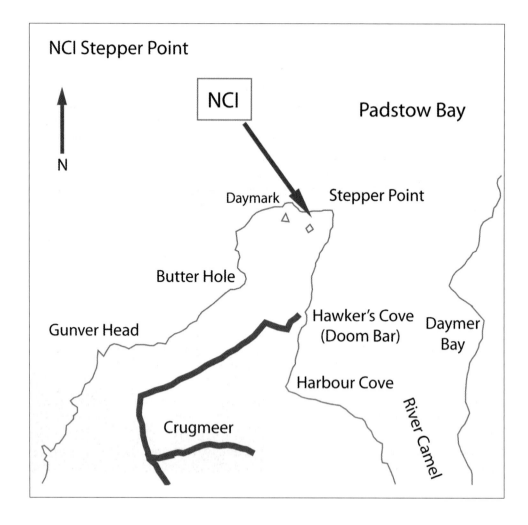

Speedboats passing in the River Camel. (Photograph Kitto Richards)

THE WATCH: TRAFFIC AND INCIDENTS

While the heyday of Padstow is long since past, it is still a working port with local and foreign trawlers and crabbers using the harbour's facilities all year round. The huge increase in waterborne leisure pursuits has been a great boost to the area, and the summer season sees a continuous passage of cruisers and yachts in and out of Padstow as well as regular excursions on the *Jubilee Queen* and the four speedboats *Jaws 2*, *Cyclone*, *Sea Fury* and *Fireball*.

Wind and kite surfers skim across the estuary, and the beaches and rocks of Daymer Bay and Polzeath are crowded with holidaymakers, all of which need to be monitored. The rocks which used to be treacherous to ships are equally dangerous to walkers.

NCI ST AGNES HEAD

Station: The Old Lookout Station,
   West Polberro, St Agnes, TR5 0ST
Tel: 01872 270431
Station Manager: Mike Pulley, 20 Polstain Crescent, Threemilestone, Truro, TR3 6DZ
   Tel: 01872 270431
Email: mikshe@talktalk.net
MCA Station: Falmouth
Website: www.nci.co.uk
Number of Volunteers: 20
Watch Hours: T.B.A.

HISTORY

Thanks to the support of the National Trust, the former coastguard shelter at St Agnes Head finally opened as an NCI station in January 2009. The old building was found to be unsafe due to its construction from mundic block, and has now been rebuilt with green credentials. It can claim to be one of the few stations to have access for people with disabilities. St Agnes Head was gifted to the National Trust by Carrick Council in May 2006. The lookout covers the thirty-seven-mile coastal area from Trevose Head in the east to Godrevy Light. It will be the twelfth NCI station in the county. Funding for the rebuilding has come from the National Trust, the Cory Environmental Trust, the Norman Family Trust, Radio Cornwall and St Agnes Local Improvements Committee. The entrance road to the station is still 'guarded' by a sentry box.

Senty post: Camp Cameron.

Cameron Camp was the home of the 10th AA Battery during the Second World War, and was used by US forces in training for D-Day.

LOCATION

50 19.02N; 005 04.35W grid SW699514

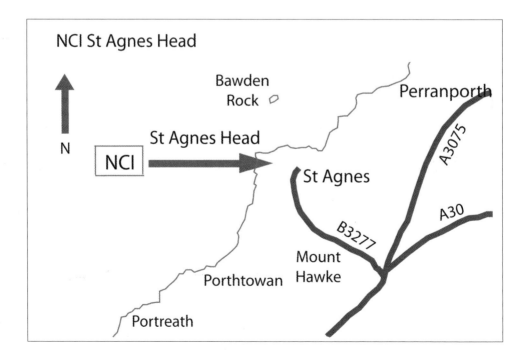

Left: C1. NCI Stepper Point. The Daymark was built by the Padstow Harbour Association in 1829 at a cost of £29. It is 254ft above sea level and was the only marker for sailors on the north coast of Cornwall before Trevose lighthouse was opened in 1847.

Below: C2. NCI Portscatho. Small but comfy: Peter Clements, station manager, on watch in the ex-coastguard station, refurbished to its original dimensions. Only slim volunteers need apply!

C3. NCI Bass Point. Honorary life membership is awarded to Mrs Maisie Culmer, mother of one of the fishermen who died below the decommissioned Bass Point coastguard station in 1994 – and led to the forming of the NCI movement. (Photograph Sue Giles)

C4. NCI Gwennap Head. A sharp-eyed watchkeeper raises the alarm and a successful aerial rescue of the unfortunate calf which had become trapped on a ledge 150ft below the cliff path was carried out.

Left: C5. NCI Charlestown. The Charlestown Harbour and Shipwreck Museum: a great attraction with three square riggers which have featured in many television and film epics.

Below: C6. NCI Stepper Point. Windsurfers in the Camel estuary are plentiful in the summer season, and need constant monitoring as they weave among the pleasure craft and speedboats. (Photograph Ness Townrow)

Above: C7. NCI Hartlepool. A spectacular picture of the Hartlepool lifeboat on call as the sea pounds the Heugh breakwater. (Photo Barry Hayton)

Below: C8. NCI Stepper Point. For centuries ships have been blown across Padstow's Doom Bar onto Greenaway Rocks. The unfortunate yacht *Fly* suffered the same fate, resisting all attempts to refloat her. (Photo Tony Davies)

C9. NCI Rame Head. From November to May, you will see several Dartmoor ponies grazing here as part of the habitat management scheme. As there are only a few original Dartmoor ponies left on the moor, the better grazing area at Rame improves the condition of the mares before breeding.

C10. NCI Portland Bill. Combined ops: helicopter *Whisky Bravo* and the Weymouth lifeboat rescuing the yacht *Palamino*.

Above: C11. NCI Bass Point. An aerial shot of the first watch station to be opened by the NCI in 1994.

Left: C12. NCI Cape Cornwall. Rough seas below one of the most exposed watch stations in the NCI. Force 12 gales are not uncommon, and on several occasions the steps to the watch are underwater.

C13. NCI Gwennap Head. A most royal occasion: HRH the Princess Royal reviewing 'the troops', having dropped in by helicopter.

C14. NCI Penzance. One of Cornwall's enduring icons, St Michael's Mount, lies three miles east of the watch station.

C15. NCI St Ives. Log that! HMS *Ark Royal* passes the watch on a courtesy visit to Cornwall.

C16. NCI Portland Bill. Another for the scrapbook: the cruise ship *Aurora* passing the Bill on her return to port after sea trials.

C17. NCI St Albans Head. One of our allies in the rescue services is the helicopter, a Sikorsky S-61N, based at Portland at the former naval station HMS *Osprey*. She has a crew of four and a capacity for thirty-five casualties.

C18. NCI Folkestone. 'At the cutting edge': soil erosion at Copt Point left the station only 5ft from disaster in 2003. Now it has been re-housed in a former Second World War gun emplacement near Martello Tower No.3 on the east cliff.

C19. NCI Teignmouth. A view from the watch station to the Ness. Calm in winter, crowded in summer.

C20 and C21. NCI Newhaven. Two spectacular photographs by watchkeeper Barry Johnson illustrate the changing weather on our coasts.

C22. NCI Mundesley. 'The Mundesley Bomb', sited next to the watch station, is a monument to the memory of the twenty-six soldiers in the bomb disposal squad (REME) who lost their lives clearing the Norfolk beaches of unexploded ordnance between 1944 and 1953.

C23. NCI Newhaven. The car ferry to Dieppe being manoeuvred into Newhaven Harbour. (Photo Barry Johnson)

C24. NCI Portland Bill. Perks of the job: a beautiful sunset seen from the watch station.

C25. NCI Wells-next-the-Sea. Survey ships moored near the old Tide House.

C26. NCI Hartlepool. The oil rig *Minerva* on tow from the harbour. (Photograph Barry Hayton)

C27. NCI Cape Cornwall. The view from the watch south to Longships lighthouse, which was first lit in 1785. On the horizon is Wolf Rock light.

C28. NCI Hartlepool. The marina festival. Rescue helicopter and Hartlepool lifeboat pictured with the *Trincomalee*. Built for the navy in Bombay in 1817, she is the oldest wooden sailing ship afloat. (Photograph Barry Hayton)

C29. NCI St Ives. A view to the watch from the harbour.

C30. NCI Felixstowe. Never a dull watch, this fire inland at the Hermann de Stern building was first spotted by watchkeeper Jim Williamson, whose pictures featured on national television and in the press.

C31. The North Cornwall coast. NCI Stepper Point and the Daymark taken from the air by watchkeeper Peter Chapman.

Above: C32. NCI Whitstable. 'The Street', a spit of land created by tidal currents, runs out a mile from the shore at low tide. (Photograph Jim Higham)

Below: C33. NCI Herne Bay. The Two Sisters, towers of the ruined church of St Mary, Reculver, have been a landmark to Thames sailors for centuries. They were last restored by Trinity House in the nineteenth century. (Photograph Jim Higham)

South Devon Region

NCI EXMOUTH

Station: The Lookout, Harbour View Café, Queens Drive, Exmouth
Tel: 01395 222492
Station Manager Bill Nash, Flat 3, Excliff, Trefusis Terr, Exmouth, EX8 2AX
Tel: 01395 28384
Email: bill.nashweb1@virgin.net
Website: www.nciexmouth.org.uk
MCA Station: Brixham
Declared Facility Status: 2006
Number of Volunteers: 52
Watch Hours: 10.00 – 18.00 (summer)   10.00 – 16.00 (winter weekends)

HISTORY

NCI Exmouth is based in a unique building, the imposing tower of the Harbour View Café. Formerly the home of the Exmouth Sailing Club, the building was originally the Bath House Café, where, in Victorian times, patrons of the fashionable Exmouth could enjoy refreshments after a visit to the health-giving salt water baths. The Admiralty Chart of 1827 indicates that a coastguard lookout stood on this site. The watch was opened on 7 January 1998.

LOCATION
50 36.789N 003 24.634W grid SY003802

NCI Exmouth stands at the mouth of the River Exe. The waters of the Exe and the open sea meet at this point, and a tidal range of 4.2m goes through the narrow channel giving unpredictable currents. A ferry from Starcross, on the far bank of the Exe, lands near a small jetty which is still used by coasters today. It is a link

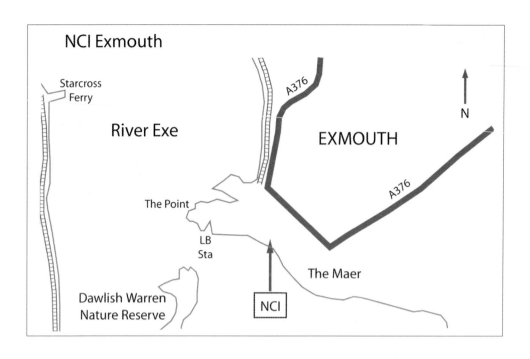

NCI Exmouth

Starcross Ferry

River Exe

A376

EXMOUTH

N

A376

The Point

LB Sta

The Maer

NCI

Dawlish Warren
Nature Reserve

Starcross Ferry.

with Exmouth's Elizabethan heyday when the town was one of Devon's most important maritime centres, used as a base by Sir Walter Raleigh.

AND FINALLY …
Don Lopez, one of our watchkeepers, has had success with his autobiography *Don Emilio*. It is the story of his life in Spain during the Spanish Civil War, and his escape to England via Gibraltar.

NCI FROWARD POINT

Station: Froward Point
Tel: 07976 505649
Station Manager: Bob Tozer, Greyholme, Bascombe
Rd, Churston Ferrers, Brixham, Devon, TQ5 0JW
Tel: 01803 844235 **Mobile:** 07990598859
Email: greyholme@talktalk.net
Website: www.nci-frowardpoint.org.uk
MCA Station: Brixham
Number of Volunteers: 50
Watch Hours: 09.00 – 17.00 (summer) 10.00 – 16.00 (winter)
  Royal Dartmouth Yacht races on Wednesday evenings.

HISTORY

The watch station is housed in the former observation post of the Brownstone Coastal Defence
Battery. In 1940 the land was requisitioned from Brownstone Farm and a coastal defence battery
was built on the site. The site was a large complex, with two ex-naval 6in guns, two searchlights,
an observation post, armoury, a railway on an inclined plane to take ammunition to the second
gun, billets for 230 soldiers of the 52nd Bedfordshire Yeomanry and a water reservoir.

A gun preserved at Pendennis Castle.

The observation post was manned
by signallers, telephonists, gun control
officers and clerks whose job was to
transmit settings and firing times to the
gun crews.

The guns were removed in 1951 and it
is something of a mystery as to their final
location. The site was decommissioned in
1956 and it is now owned by the National
Trust from whom it is leased.

In 2002 the idea of having a visual
watch was mooted and by 2004 a group
of volunteers had taken on the task of
turning the very overgrown observation
post into a functioning station and
repairing the mile-long access road. Watch
training began in April 2005, and in June
eleven engineers from Hawke Division,
Britannia Royal Naval College, did two
days of major work on the site, including
installing the generator. The first watch
was opened in July.

LOCATION
50 20.20N; 003 32.58W grid SX903496

Froward Point stands at the eastern side of the River Dart estuary, commanding views over Start Bay. With 2,800 boats registered on the Dart the station is always busy.

THE WATCH: TRAFFIC AND INCIDENTS

In common with several NCI stations, Froward Point is situated on the south-west coastal path. It is also in an area of outstanding natural beauty. Some time ago National Trust placed a counter on a nearby stretch of the coast path and recorded over 30,000 users in less than twelve months. Dartmouth has a fishing fleet, mainly potters, which pass within a mile of the station on a daily basis. The Brixham pilot station, some four miles to the east, brings large commercial vessels, bulk carriers, auto-transporters, etc. close enough to be easily identified. Brixham still has a large trawler fleet which is logged regularly, and together with the huge popularity of Dartmouth with pleasure boaters, both sail and power, the station is very busy, especially in summer. The Dartmouth Royal Regatta attracts many visitors. Canoeists are also a source of anxiety as they circle the Mewstone Rocks in front of the station some 500m offshore.

An incident logged:

On Wednesday 28th September the duty watchkeepers were asked, on logging in with Brixham coastguard at 09:00 hrs, if they could see a steel-hulled catamaran, the *Jose Jacqueline*. Its reported position was a little over quarter of a mile south of the Mewstone rock. It had requested assistance

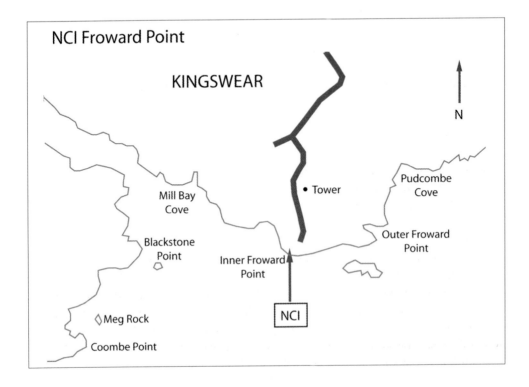

A rare event: the *Seven Seas Voyager* passes the watch.

as it had suffered engine failure, and was drifting towards the rocks. Torbay lifeboat and a coastguard mobile unit had been tasked to the incident, and the fishing vessel *Bosloe* in the River Dart had volunteered to assist, as it could reach the casualty very quickly.

No vessel could be seen in the reported position, but a registered fishing vessel appeared to be working very close to the rocks extending west from the Mewstone.

Its registered number was clearly visible, and on checking the station's fishing vessel reference information, it was found that this was in fact the *Jose Jacqueline*. It is a workboat used in connection with mussel beds, and does indeed have a catamaran-type hull, though this is not apparent from most angles of view!

This information was passed to the coastguard, together with the information that it was now very close to the rocks. It had drifted very quickly with the fresh to strong onshore wind.

Fortunately the crew managed to deploy an anchor, which slowed the rate of drift, and the fishing vessel *Bosloe* was able to pass a line, and start towing her out to sea before the casualty struck. A little later the coastguard mobile unit arrived at the watch station to assess the situation. Then the Torbay lifeboat arrived and took over the tow, transferring the casualty to the quay in Kingswear. No damage had been sustained, but it was a very close call!

NCI PRAWLE POINT

Station: NCI Prawle Point, Po Box 58, Kingsbridge, Devon, TQ7 2ZQ
Tel: 01548 511259
Station Manager: Roger Barrett, Higher Oddicombe Barn, Chillington, Kingsbridge, TQ7 2JD
Tel: 01548 531167
Email: rogbarett@aol.com
Website: prawlepoint@ex-parrot.com
MCA Station: Brixham
Declared Facility Status: 2000
Number of Volunteers: 60
Watch Hours: 09.00 – 17.00 (winter) 09.00 – 21.00 (summer)

HISTORY

The present lookout building is believed to have been built by the Admiralty as a coastguard watch house in the 1860s. The name 'prawle' is the Old English word for lookout. It became a Lloyds signal station in 1882, and from here Lloyds signalmen telegraphed details of passing merchant ships to Lloyds of London, for the benefit of anxious owners and underwriters (today the NCI watchkeepers at Prawle Point still perform this role, sending details of passing ships to Lloyds by fax). Between 1903 and 1956 Lloyds signalling at Prawle was undertaken by naval personnel, and Prawle Point was designated a Royal Naval shore signal station or, in wartime, a

war signal station. When the coastguard service transferred to the Board of Trade in 1926, Prawle Point remained under Admiralty control, but the men stationed here also performed coastguard duties. In 1956 the Prawle Point station was finally handed over to HM Coastguard. By the late 1960s constant twenty-four-hour watch was being maintained by five regular officers and six auxiliaries. However, the growing use of VHF radio for distress signalling led to a steady reduction in visual watchkeeping and, from 1982, the lookout was manned only intermittently by the local Auxiliary Rescue Company for 'foul weather watches'. Closure finally came in 1994.

In May 1997 retired sea captains John Chapple and Christopher Trinick saw the potential in restoring the abandoned lookout to form Devon's first NCI station. Whilst it had been closed the familiar landmark above the point had become semi-derelict and open to the elements. It had a leaking roof and broken doors and windows, and there was no water, sewerage, electricity or equipment. However, with the help of generous funding from local people, companies and bodies, it was transformed into a well-equipped and efficient working station. John Baverstock, Jonathan Ansell and John Erskine were among the first to undertake the formidable task of refurbishing and equipping the lookout after the lease had been agreed with the National Trust, the landowners, in 1997. Essential roof re-slating was carried out by local contractors, but the remainder of the work was carried out, in all weathers, by the volunteers. In October 1997 and May 1998 further help came from Raleigh International volunteers from Oxford who set up camp in the village.

Regular watchkeeping was resumed at the lookout on 5 April 1998 when the NCI Prawle Point station opened. Once operational, the station was manned by a team of thirty volunteer watchkeepers led by Station Manager Jonathan Ansell. Jonathan, who had lived and worked within sight of the lookout for almost all his life, was a member of the Cliff Rescue and Auxiliary Coastguard teams and a former mate on the former Brixham trawler and ICC training vessel, *Provident*.

In the spring of 2000, after assessment by Brixham Coastguard, Prawle Point achieved Declared Facility Status. In the following year, further substantial improvements were made to the lookout. Thanks to generous donations of £30,000 from Sir Donald Gosling, £4,000 from the Cyrus Clark Trust, £4,000 from South Hams District Council and £12,000 from other local supporters, it was possible to extend the lookout westward. As a result, the operational area was extended to Salcombe Bar and working conditions were greatly improved. Between July and November 2001, whilst the extension was under construction, watchkeeping was maintained in a wooden shed safely bolted and wired down against the elements. On 18 June

2002 Captain Sir Donald Gosling RNR, the guest of honour at the official opening of the rebuilt lookout, arrived by helicopter, to be greeted by the NCI chairman, Jon Gifford, and a gathering of supporters, watchkeepers, friends and families.

In summer 2002, Derrick Yeoman took over as station manager. At the time Derrick had chalked up forty-two years of watching out for others at sea. A founder member and chairman, in 1960, of the Bantham Surf Life Saving Club, he became a part-time beach safety officer for the local council in 1972, and an auxiliary coastguard in Hope Cove in 1974, assisting in rescues there for the next seventeen years. Under his leadership, the NCI Prawle Point station has grown in strength, and now, in 2006, a fully trained team of some sixty volunteers turn out in all weather conditions to keep the station open 365 days a year. Between them they keep watch between 9.00. and 17.00, with an additional evening watch between 17.00. and 21.00. during the summer months.

LOCATION
50 12.17N 003 43.22W grid SX773351

Prawle Point is Devon's southernmost extremity. Projecting into the English Channel between Bolt Head to the west and Start Point to the east, its lofty promontory, 200ft above sea level, has served as a vantage point since ancient times and, appropriately enough, 'the prawle', as already mentioned, is an old English word meaning 'lookout'. A chapel dedicated to St Brendan may well have stood here in medieval times, on the site of the present watch house, and, during the Napoleonic Wars an Admiralty signal station was sited nearby.

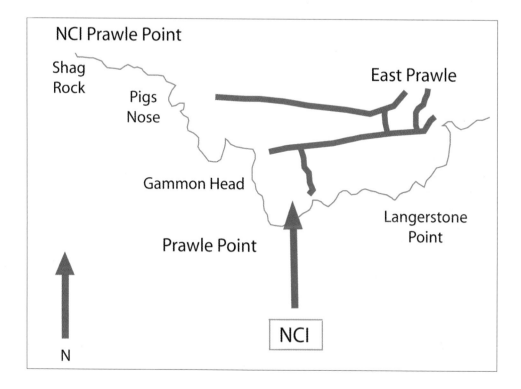

The rocks below Prawle Point have seen the destruction of nine recorded ships, including the wreck of the 9,700-ton cargo ship *Demetrius* in 1992.

Watchkeepers maintain a visual guard of the waters between Start Point and Bolt Head, and beyond, logging all identifiable craft passing below the station. Their priority is to keep a sharp look-out for vulnerable craft such as small sailing boats, open boats, divers and onshore walkers and sea anglers. During eight years of operation NCI Prawle Point watchkeepers have reported numerous incidents to Brixham Coastguard involving, for instance, missing divers, de-masted yachts, engine breakdowns, fouled propellers, upturned dinghies and injured walkers. In their role as 'eyes along the coast' they have undoubtedly made an important contribution to the safety of people and craft venturing along the South Hams coast.

Three incidents on one afternoon illustrate the work of the watch:

On the way to the lookout a man was observed waving with both arms from a rocky outcrop. While it transpired that he was waving to a friend he was gently reminded that his action was a distress signal and could have triggered a rescue incident.

During the afternoon a walker heard cries for help from a young woman who had fallen down a 200ft cliff to a ledge below. The watchkeepers alerted Brixham coastguard and the subsequent rescue involved the Prawle mobile rescue team, a West Country ambulance, and a coastguard rescue helicopter. The lady was successfully transported to a hospital in Plymouth.

The afternoon ended with a report of a sheep over the cliff at Elender Cove. This was reported by a walker but the sheep was never traced.

Unsurprisingly, the lookout is not connected to either the mains water or sewerage. Being on the top of a hill the possibilities of a natural water source are also non-existent. This means that all of the water used must either be rain collected from the roof or carried up from the old coastguard cottages, 500 yards horizontally and about 100ft vertically. This leads to an altogether different appreciation of water.

NCI TEIGNMOUTH

Station: Old Coastguard Lookout, Eastcliff Walk, Teignmouth, TQ14 8SH
Tel: 01626 772377
Station Manager: Anne Channing, 9 Ashleigh Mount, Teignmouth, TQ14 8QU
Tel: 01626 778776
Email: ajcthomas@fsmail.net
Website: www.nci.org.uk/stations
MCA Station: Brixham/Portland
Number of Volunteers: 40
Watch Hours: 10.00 – 18.00 (summer) 10.00 – 16.00 (winter)
    Seven days per week plus Christmas and New Year's Day

HISTORY

The founding of NCI Teignmouth owes a great deal to its neighbouring NCI station at Exmouth. In summer of 2004, John Langford, the station manager of Exmouth, happened to be in Teignmouth for the day when he noticed the vacant coastguard lookout at Eastcliff. He set in motion the negotiations which led to the leasing of the building to the NCI. The official opening day was 25 May 2005, and a cheque for £1,000 was given by the Mayor of Teignmouth, Cllr Mary Strudwick. Despite a setback in early 2006 when the lookout was ransacked by vandals, the town rallied to the cause and donations were made by the Cooperative Society, the town council, the Rotary Club and the Regatta Committee. 'The volunteers do a great job looking after us so we wanted to help them,' was the byword of the day. Teignmouth now has forty volunteers and is managed by Anne Channing, one of the only two woman NCI station managers.

LOCATION

50 32.907 N 003 29.455 W grid SX945732

NCI Teignmouth is situated overlooking Eastcliff beach to the north of the Teign estuary, and monitors one mile of sea wall, a jet ski and powerboat lane and an EEC-designated bathing beach (see colour section, picture 23).

THE WATCH: TRAFFIC AND INCIDENTS

The watch monitors a wide range of traffic over the year, from commercial fishing boats and charter vessels (fishing, diving and sightseeing) to local and international gig and seine boat racing, sailing dingy events and power boat racing. Day boats, jet skis and inflatables also keep us on our toes. Examples of recent incidents include:

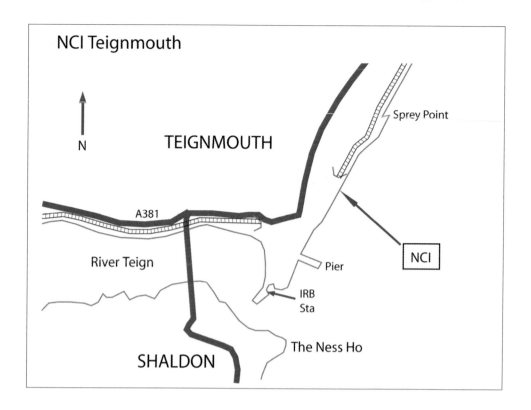

04/08/05 Three teenage girls spotted by watch clinging to the capsized jet ski 200 yards off Eastcliffe beach. Brixham CG notified and ILB tasked to pick up girls.

14/08/05 Casualty brought in to NCI lookout with head injury. Ambulance called. Teign lifeguard tasked to assist with the help of Teignmouth Coastguard. Oxygen administered. Casualty released.

01/04/06 20ft day boat reported to be in trouble in Labrador Bay. Brixham coastguard notified. Boat waiting for better sea conditions. Alert stood down.

30/09/06 Jet ski ran aground – hull punctured and sinking. Towed by second jet ski. Tow rope snapped and both overturned. ILB and mobile CG on scene. Three occupants OK, crafts taken to shore.

Dorset Region

NCI PEVERIL POINT

Station: NCI Lookout, Peveril Point, Swanage, Dorset
Tel: 01929 422596
Email: nci-peveril@lineone.net
Station Manager: Ian Surface, 5 Cowlease, Swanage, Dorset, BH19 2QE
Tel: 01929 425405
Email: isurface@aol.com
Website: www.purbeck-dc.gov.uk
MCA Station: Weymouth
Watch Hours: 10.00 – 19.00 (all year)

HISTORY

The coastguard station at Peveril Point was built in 1964 and, following the closure of visual watches by the coastguard, the site was taken over by the NCI in 1994. The initial problem was that the building was in such a dilapidated state that it had to be completely rebuilt before it could house the watch.

The work, funded by the Millenium Project, was planned and supervised by Station Manager Ian Surface, supported by a team of volunteers. The erection of the new lookout took seven weeks, preceded by a good deal of prefabrication at a local workshop in Swanage. Its unique design has seven windows sloping inward on a steel frame. The new station is now well equipped thanks to fund-raising efforts by the team and donations from Swanage Coastal Protection Association and Swanage Town Council. It was officially opened on 15 September 2001.

LOCATION
50 36.43N 001 56.69W grid SZ 041787

Peveril Point overlooks Durlston Bay to the south and Swanage Bay to the north, famed for Alfred the Great's reputed victory over the Danes in AD 877.

Left: NCI Peveril Point befoe upgrading. (Watchkeeper)

Opposite: Swanage lifeboat.

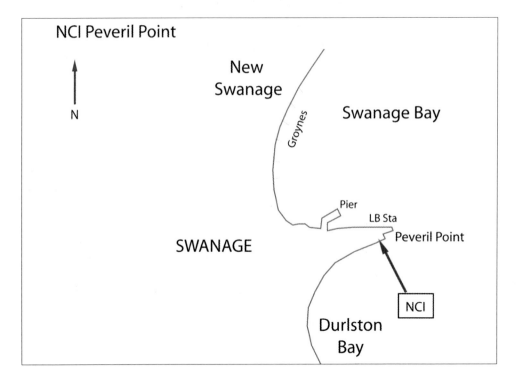

To dispel any doubts, local worthy John Mowlem built a monument to commemorate this event, a column topped with cannonballs fired from the English fleet at the Crimea.

THE WATCH: TRAFFIC AND INCIDENTS

On 30 June 2006 the watch had been observing a dinghy with a single occupant since 15.00. At 15.30, at full ebb tide, the vessel was at three nautical miles and in danger of being becalmed. It was apparent the helmsman was a novice from the erratic steering of the boat. The boom, swinging from side to side, appeared on one occasion to strike the man on the head. One hour

later he was becalmed and began to row, unaware that the tide was taking him further from safety. At 16.30 the helmsman tacked to the west but the tide was running faster than the wind could push him. At 16.45 a French sloop spotted him and offered a tow, which was accepted. The dinghy seemed out of danger now except that his only way back to Swanage was through the tide race. At 17.00, as the watch was due to stand down, HMG Portland was informed of the incident and requested that NCI stay on watch and observe. The ILB was launched and the dinghy towed back to Swanage.

Peveril NCI had done its job – making sure that the incident was contained and the safety of those involved assured.

NCI PORTLAND BILL

Station: NCI Lookout, Old Higher Lighthouse Rd, Portland Bill
Tel: 01305 860178
Station Manager: Geoff Peters, Sandbanks, Furzy Close, Preston, Weymouth, DT3 6RX
Tel: 01305 837216
Email: geoff@petersg.fsbusiness.net
Website: www.Coastwatch-online.org.uk/stations
MCA Station: Portland
Number of Volunteers: 50
Watch Hours: 07.00. – 19.00

HISTORY

The lookout at Portland Bill was built in 1934 and operated by HM Coastguard as a full-time (twenty-four hour) station. In the 1970s it was manned by auxiliaries and the hours gradually reduced until finally it was open only during daylight hours. During the reorganisation of the MCA it was closed along with other visual lookouts and earmarked for demolition. The story goes that a local fisherman, Ken Lynham, was walking his dog near the lookout when the JCB arrived to begin the demolition. Ken, being a member of the Southern Fishermen's Association, knew about the formation of the NCI and its work in reopening coastguard lookouts, and so he stepped into the path of the oncoming digger and stopped the destruction of the lookout. Ken then contacted the NCI who agreed to take the lookout on and Auxiliary Coastguard David Crabb, the current president, who was originally based at the station, agreed to take on the task of refurbishing the station and getting volunteers. Initial funding was given by the Weymouth Trawler Race, but the big breakthrough came when Eagle Star Insurance, through their subsidiary Navigators & General, gave a substantial grant of £11,750. The station was officially opened on 23 May 1997.

Coming to the present, the lookout was seventy years old in 2004. It was cramped with room for only two watchkeepers, cold in winter, and leaky! The committee, under Station Manager Peter Neville, undertook to raise funds for the complete modernisation of the building. £70,000 was raised, and the 'new' lookout was reopened on 24 April, and officially opened on 27 July 2004 when it was blessed by the station's chaplain, the Revd Anita Thorne.

LOCATION
50 31.28N 002 27.45W grid SY 676692

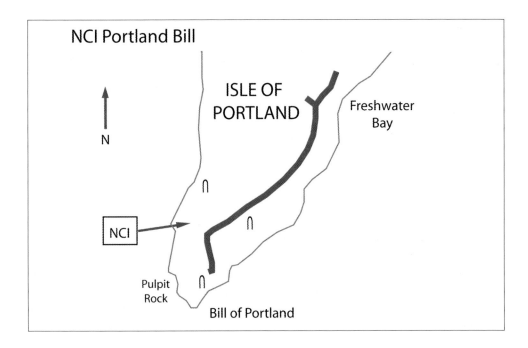

NCI Portland Bill

ISLE OF PORTLAND

Freshwater Bay

N

NCI

Pulpit Rock

Bill of Portland

We are located approximately 50m above sea level at the southern end of the Isle of Portland. Our field of view is on a good day fifteen nautical miles to the horizon, and on an exceptional day we can see, looking east, the westerly tip of the Isle of Wight, and looking west the two radio masts behind Paignton. We have a 360 degree view so, as well as shipping, we also keep watch on the coastal path, climbers on the cliff, and have even reported fires in Weymouth to the fire brigade.

One story we tell is of a woman horse riding by the lookout when the horse was spooked by a dog and she was thrown from it. The horse then kicked her, breaking her leg. The watch consisted of a farmer, an ex-paramedic and an 'ordinary' person. The paramedic attended to the woman, the farmer caught and tended to the horse and the other watchkeeper alerted the emergency services. We always say that we cannot guarantee to have the right combination on every watch. Our main concern is the Portland Race which is caused by the tidal flow between the Shambles Bank and the ledges at the tip of Portland. These restrictions create fast-flowing water which, when it meets the various ledges and other sand banks, forces the water upwards to form turbulent patches of water. Because the race moves according to the state of tide, the unwary yachtsman/woman can be easily caught out as they round the Bill travelling east to west.

THE WATCH: TRAFFIC AND INCIDENTS

Our traffic is seasonal with potters and inshore fishing vessels local to Weymouth all the year round, with angling and dive charters, and local pleasure craft, mainly during the summer months.

We have commercial shipping using Portland Port, and this is on the increase, as is RFA and RN use, especially with the port being considered for nuclear submarines. We also monitor aircraft such as RN Lynx and Merlin helicopters plus the SAR helicopter *Whisky Bravo* (see colour section, picture 10) and fixed-wing craft such as Dassault Falcon 20s from Bournemouth International Airport, as well as RAF Nimrods exercising in the area. In the summer it is quite common to record forty shipping movements in a four-hour watch, with sometimes 100-plus in a four-hour watch on the weekend.

Two incidents from the log illustrate perfectly the role of NCI Portland Bill:

Renee Skilleter was on watch when she was called by mobile at 8.10 by the captain of a vessel which had broken down in the SW shipping lanes, not only losing all power but all radio contact as well. Despite his difficulty with English and his understandable distress, Renee managed to get his vessel details, *Gambler*, V2ATS, at 50.08.06 N 002.02.09 W, which she sent to Portland CG and ensured that the captain kept his mobile switched on so that he could be contacted.

On a foul day in February 2006 with the wind gusting from Force 6, a Shetland-type cabin cruiser was observed with 2 pov. The watch questioned immediately why such a small boat was out in these conditions? The answer came quickly when Portland CG requested any sightings of a small boat which was wanted by the police having been stolen from Christchurch with a possible illegal immigrant on board. The watch gave the vessel's description and carried out a watching brief. Dorset police now requested a situation report which was given and Helicopter and Lifeboat were tasked to attend. The cruiser was subsequently towed to West Bay where the skipper was arrested. A copy of the watch log was requested by the police.

AND FINALLY...

The Mayor of Portland, Tim Woodcock, was so impressed with the work of the watch that he asked if he could join the team. He started in January 2006, along with seven other recruits. Is Portland the first to recruit a mayor?

ST ALBAN'S HEAD

Station: NCI Lookout, St Aldhelm's (or St Alban's) Head, Worth Matravers, Dorset
Tel: 01929 439220.
Station Manager: Chris Quarrie, Hunters Moon, Streetway Lane, Cheselbourne, DT2 7NT
Tel: 01305 848787
Email: euroglen@btinternet.com
Website: www.nci-st-albans.org.uk
MCA Station: Portland Coastguard, Weymouth
Declared Facility Status: December 2005
Number of Volunteers: 30
Watch Hours: 10.00 - 17.00 (local time) every day except for Christmas Day

HISTORY

HM Coastguard's first station in the area was at the nearby Chapman's Pool and moved to St Aldhelm's Head in 1895 where a new lookout, equipment store and four cottages had been built (close to where we are currently situated). In later years the families found the cottages to be too remote and new cottages and a store were built in nearby Weston in the early 1950s. This 'new' store is still in use today by the local auxiliary coastguard unit. One of three NCI stations in Dorset, the present lookout was constructed for HM Coastguard in the 1970s, and when the coastguard service ceased to man visual lookouts in 1994, the building was returned to the landowners, the Encombe Estate. The lookout is now owned by the Scott Trust and leased to the NCI on a peppercorn rent of £1 per annum.

The NCI facility here was opened in May 1995, thanks to the efforts of Mr Graham Roff, as a sub-station of Peveril Point, Swanage. It became independent the following summer, and achieved Declared Facility Status in December 2005. For the first three years after going it alone, Sunseeker International most generously provided sponsorship. In the summer of 2006 the station was given an Awards For All grant by

St Alban's finest.

the National Lottery of £7,467, and this allowed for a major refurbishment of the building and the upgrading of some of our equipment that autumn. The station reopened on 4 December 2006 with – in addition to the existing radio and radar equipments – an electronic chart display and a shipping Automatic Information System (AIS), a more efficient and 'user-friendly' layout of working surfaces and reference material which, with the main binoculars mounted on a full-span rail, eliminated previous blind spots.

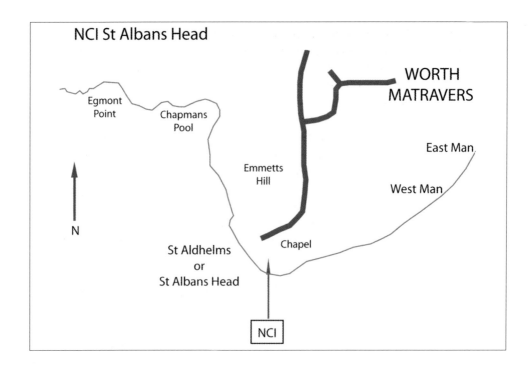

NCI St Albans Head

Egmont Point
Chapmans Pool
WORTH MATRAVERS
East Man
Emmetts Hill
West Man
N
St Aldhelms
or
St Albans Head
Chapel
NCI

LOCATION
50 34.8 N 002 03.3 W grid SY961755

The station is located 335ft (102m) above sea level on the World Heritage Jurassic Coast, roughly equidistant between the major pleasure and commercial ports of Poole to the east and Weymouth and Portland to the west, and we concentrate on the area from Anvil Point with its lighthouse (which produces a white flash every ten seconds) in the east, to Mupe Rocks at Worbarrow Bay westward, and seaward, up to five nautical miles. On a clear day views extend as far as to the Isle of Wight and Portland. The headland is the southernmost point on the mainland Dorset coastline (although not as far south as Portland Bill on its peninsular, at the end of the Chesil beach). Immediately below the station is the notorious St Alban's Race.

The site is also a haven for wildlife, most especially migrants, seabirds and cliff dwellers. To name but a very few, we have the pleasure of watching peregrine falcons, buzzards, fulmars, swallows, martins and swifts and, in spring and autumn, numerous warblers, wheatears and other passerine types on passage to and from warmer climes well to the south of the British Isles. When a chough was spotted nearby, dozens of birdwatchers descended on the headland to add this rarity (in Dorset) to their sightings lists. The odd fox and roe deer occasionally pass by, and we pass details of any dolphins seen in the waters below to the Dolphin Watch.

THE WATCH: TRAFFIC AND INCIDENTS
Our main 'trade' consists of the numerous pleasure craft which pass below us, often on passage between Weymouth or Portland and Poole, whilst diving boats and fishing boats are also routinely in our waters. Most commercial traffic is seaward of our area of prime interest, but

shipping entering Poole Harbour crosses our eastern boundary, and it is quite common to see RIBS from the Royal Marine Centre at Hamworthy racing by. Royal Naval and NATO warships and vessels of the Royal Fleet Auxiliary are also regularly logged.

An important further role is acting as a pair of eyes for the control centre on the army ranges, particularly close inshore. Shellfire isn't planned to enter the sea, but ricochets above the coastal hills sometimes do occur and a danger area exists to protect shipping offshore, and is patrolled by water-jet-driven range safety launches. We also keep a weather eye on ramblers and hikers of varying grades of age, fitness and preparedness (we are located alongside the Dorset coastal footpath), climbers and occasional hang-gliders. Our location on the footpath is advantageous to our fund-raising, and those walking dogs are especially pleased to see our two 'doggie water bowls' on hot days, and are normally willing to dig into their pockets!

We have a good working relationship with Portland coastguard and, as would be expected, have acted as their eyes and, at times, ears on our thinly populated stretch of the Dorset coastline. On numerous occasions watchkeepers have been able to visually identify casualties in radio contact only with the coastguard and assist with the rapid passage to an accurate datum of the rescue units despatched to their assistance. Amongst the more interesting events in which the duty personnel at the lookout have usefully participated was an incident when two divers became separated from their safety boat when thick fog rapidly descended on their dive site and it was possible to aurally track them as they passed by the station in a strong tide by assessing the changing bearings of the emergency whistles on their lifejackets. On other occasions pleasure craft lost in fog off the headland have been identified by radar, with this information being passed by telephone to the coastguard for relaying to the craft.

In a style reminiscent of the coastguard service of yesteryear, one August morning red flares from a de-masted catamaran were seen offshore and the coastguard was alerted, resulting in the launching of the Swanage lifeboat and a safe tow to port for the catamaran. Our monitoring of Channel 16 resulted in a Pan Pan call being intercepted which had not been detected by any other agency, and a yacht with collapsed rigging being attended upon by both the coastguard s-61n helicopter and the Swanage and Poole lifeboats, whilst on another occasion an object in the water which could have been an upturned life raft was spotted, but the s-61n's crew were able to confirm that it was just some maritime wreckage. A good pair of eyes on another day spotted the helmsman thrown from his rib craft in the St Alban's Race, and the duty watchkeeper was able to assist in the rapid vectoring to the craft, into which the helmsman had by now been recovered, of a passing RNLI craft and the helicopter.

Maybe one of the best examples of what can be done by a well-prepared NCI watchkeeper occurred when we were able to use our then recently installed radar to home the Swanage lifeboat, via a telephone line to HM Coastguard, on to the disabled yacht *Cambria Star* which the lifeboat was having difficulty locating in the thick fog which had reduced visibility to just 200m. The yacht had fouled her propeller two miles offshore, but was then towed to safety by the lifeboat, while the St Alban's Head mobile team stood by ashore.

The main search and rescue assets working in our area, in addition to the auxiliary coastguard units, are the sea-going lifeboats based at Weymouth and Swanage, and the coastguard helicopter from Portland. Weymouth is equipped with a Severn-class lifeboat 17-32 *Ernest and Mabel*, and Swanage boasts a Mersey-class vessel 12-23 *Robert Charles Brown*. Both stations are also equipped with IRBs.

Weymouth lifeboat.

The helicopter is a Sikorksy s-61N with state-of-the-art equipment, 6ft longer than the better known Sea King, with a crew of four: two pilots, a winchman and a winch operator. On standby twelve hours each day of the year (09.00-21.00 hours), it has a range of some 400 nautical miles, an endurance of four hours, a top speed of 131 knots (150mph) and a maximum capacity of thirty-five casualties (see colour section, picture 20). The s-61 based at Portland is normally G-BPWB, which is housed in a new hangar on the site of the former naval air station HMS *Osprey*, and all of these assets together with the land-based units are held in very high regard by the local population, be they seagoing folk or not. Very occasionally an RAF Nimrod MR2 will appear in the local area on an SAR mission, usually well offshore but within good Channel 16 reception range.

South East Region

NCI FOLKESTONE

Station: NCI Lookout, Copt Point, Folkestone, Kent
Tel: 01303 227132
Station Manager (Acting): Tony Hutt, Rosewood Cott, 18 Canterbury Rd, Hawkinge,
   Kent, CT18 7BW
Tel: 01303 891102
Email: tony.hutt@virgin.net
Website: www.members.lycos.co.uk/loel
MCA Station: Dover
Declared Facility Status: 2000, re-awarded 2004
Number of Volunteers: 52
Watch Hours: 10.00 – 18.00 (summer)   09.00 – 17.00 (winter, or sunset)

HISTORY

A coastguard station existed at Copt Point from the early nineteenth century. The first 'station' was in fact a purposely breached brig, *Pelter*, used as part of the coast blockade, the forerunner of the coastguard, against smuggling.

NCI Folkestone was set up in spring 1998 by John Mills-Baker, an ex-merchant navy skipper, and officially opened on 10 October that year. The abandoned coastguard lookout at Copt Point was leased from Shepway District Council. In the early days the station operated at weekends only. John Mills-Baker then moved to become regional manager, so Chris Hutchison became station manager, putting in much hard work prior to the award of Declared Facility Status on 25 July 2000. Under the management of Bev Sheppard, the current manager, the station has over fifty members and in March 2002 was able to mount a full watch seven days a week.

Coastal erosion, in particular the collapse of part of the cliffs in the area of Copt Point, has kept the watchkeepers 'on the move' over the past five years. Following the first cliff fall in 2001, which left the station standing initially 8ft from the edge, finally narrowing to become only 54in, it was eventually decided to abandon the post in January 2003 and move to the nearby

Martello Tower (see colour section, picture 21). This was a temporary relief, but with access only gained by climbing an outside stairway and then a narrow, stone stairway to the roof-top observation room with very restricted views from where the watch was carried out, the tower was deemed unsatisfactory in the longer term. In the summer of 2003 a steel portakabin was purchased and, after several weeks of hard work, was made operational. A landline was provided by BT and the station purchased a generator and a butane heater. The all important cuppa was brewed on a camp stove.

In 2006 there came a third and hopefully final move to the former Second World War gun emplacement on the east cliff adjacent to the Martello Tower No.3. The council offered to lease the facility to the NCI, and a massive £47,000 for the refurbishment was raised by various fund-raising events together with a generous donation from Kent County Council and local businesses. The fact that the portakabin lease expired in March 2006 also concentrated the mind to get the station up and running, and this took place on 12 April 2006.

LOCATION
51 05.06N; 001 11.91E grid TR241366

The station is located on the golf course on Wear Bay Road next to Martello Tower No.3. It overlooks the English Channel and is 50m above sea level. To the west there is a clear view of Folkestone Harbour, while to the east is Dover – the busiest ferry port in the world. Just south are the ventilation shafts of a Royal Observer Corp's underground post, dating from the Cold War period, and two concrete and brick gun emplacements used to defend the coast against Hitler's possible invasion force.

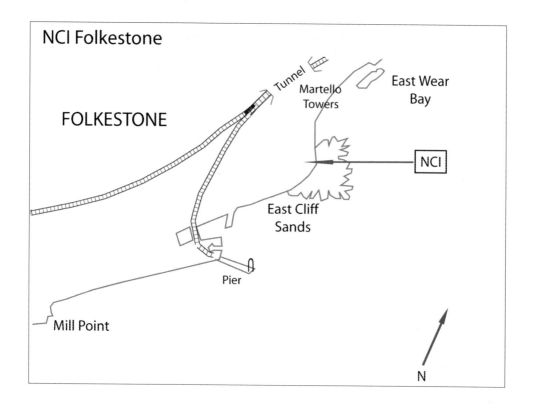

NCI Folkestone

THE WATCH: TRAFFIC AND INCIDENTS

Folkestone Harbour lost its cross-Channel traffic some years ago and is now mainly used by the local fishing fleet, yachtsmen and commercial vessels. A range of services provided by the port include a ro-ro facility and hazardous handling. The port can take vessels up to 130m in length with a dead weight of 2,000 tons.

We monitor and record all traffic in and out of the harbour and note their heading on leaving. In the summer 'silly' season we also keep watch over two main pleasure beach areas, keeping an eye out for swimmers, kite surfers, canoeists and dive boats, as well as fossil hunters on the beach and children on lilos who could drift out to sea. We also monitor cliff walkers and youths who set fire to abandoned cars and push them over the cliff onto the main Folkestone–Dover railway line (when this happened in 2002 we were able to telephone the railway police and have the trains stopped pending investigation).

Around high tide, in reasonable weather, there could be twenty or more movements by commercial fishing vessels, and very little else in the winter. In summer there are also many movements by fishing charter vessels and small, privately owned cruisers, motor boats and yachts, and at weekends these could amount to forty or more log entries in a four-hour watch.

AND FINALLY...

Being the nearest station to Europe, it is fitting that Folkestone has some members fluent in French, Dutch, German and Norwegian. Two visitors from Hong Kong were a little surprised, however, when watchkeeper Laurie Bruce conversed with them in perfect Cantonese!

NCI WHITSTABLE

Station: Marine Crescent, Tankerton Slopes, Whitstable, Kent
Tel: 07961 968707
Station Manager: Julie Skinner, 74 Ingoldsby Rd, Birchington, Kent, CT7 9PJ
Tel: 01843 842891
Email: seagul12string@aol.com
Website: www.nci.org.uk/stations
MCA Station: Walton on the Naze
Number of Volunteers: 20
Watch Hours: 10.00 - 17.00 (Sundays and Bank Holidays)

HISTORY

NCI Whitstable was formed when, in spring 2003, several members from neighbouring Herne Bay thought it would be a good idea if a branch was set up further along the coast. The first watches were kept from a mobile caravan on Tankerton Slopes. Next, Canterbury Council loaned a beach hut, rent free, at the top of Tankerton Slopes, which gave a better vantage point and better views of the coast.

Eventually, through various fund-raising events and donations, we raised money to purchase a beach hut with a 180-degree view, and the new lookout was opened in August 2006. The present location is excellent as it gives the general public a chance to meet the watchkeepers and discover more about the NCI.

LOCATION

51 21.9N; 001 03.6E grid TR167613

NCI Whitstable is situated east of the harbour in the district of Tankerton. The lookout stands behind Tankerton beach at the foot of the steep grass bank called Tankerton Slopes.

The slopes form an important part of town life and in midsummer they host the Whitstable Regatta, a two-day event staged over a weekend. The slopes are a natural theatre for a host of air and sea displays, crowned by a fireworks display on the closing night. The watch also looks out over 'the street', a narrow shingle bank which runs out into the Thames estuary, where the unwary holidaymaker can be cut off by the tide (see colour section).

Tankerton Slopes. (Photogrph Jim Higham)

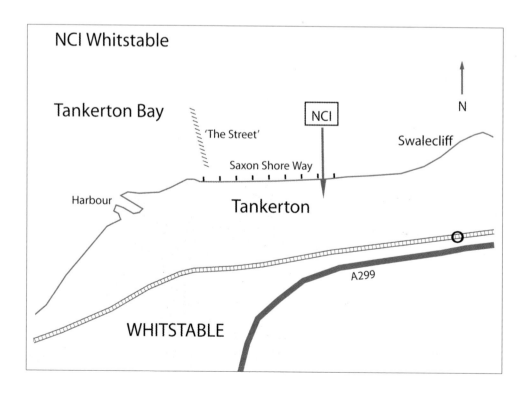

The main traffic logged are passing container ships. The paddle steamer *Waverley* is often seen during the summer months passing from Margate to Tower Bridge via a stop at Whitstable.

The revamped Thames sailing barge *Greta* takes visitors out to the forts which, during the Second World War, were manned with anti-aircraft guns. These days they are always a topic of interest for visitors to Tankerton Bay and Whitstable. Sundays usually see the Tankerton Bay Sailing Club, kite surfers and jet skis. Occasionally power boat racing has taken place. However, they have their own safety teams. The local WASP vessel (Water and Shore Patrol) usually passes en route from Herne Bay to Whitstable.

NCI HERNE BAY

Station: The Old Bathing Station, Sea Front, Herne Bay, Kent
Tel: 01227 743208
Email: nci.org
Station Manager: Wilf Heckley, 48 Mill Lane, Herne Bay, Kent
Tel: 01227 373093
Email: wildot@tiscali.com
Website: NCIHBOK
MCA Station: Thames
Number of Volunteers: 30
Watch Hours: 09.00 - 17.00 (to 16.00 in winter)

HISTORY
NCI Herne Bay was formed in 1998 with the initial intention of reopening the Bishopstone lookout which had been abandoned by the coastguard in the 1980s. Unfortunately, due to the instability of the cliffs, the building was declared unsafe and demolished by Canterbury County Council in 1999. However, the flagpole was salvaged for future use! Without a base, but having recruited a number of volunteers, training was started in the committee room of the Herne Bay Angling Association. Eventually a permanent home was found on the Eastern Esplanade. The building was described in the lease as 'the first floor premises over the public conveniences'. The building itself has its own history. A reinforced concrete structure dating from the 1900s, the ground floor was a beach toilet and beach shelter whilst the upper floor was a ladies changing station – hence our postal address. This then became a beach café, a defence establishment during the Second World War, a base for the swimming club and, prior to the NCI occupation, a windsurfers' store. Much work has gone into the transformation of a derelict structure to a purpose-built station. £3,000 of funds raised have been used to fit a new ceiling and electrical installation. A watch room 16ft x 8ft has been built with laminated glass in the sea-facing windows which also have protective motorised shutters.

LOCATION
51 22.4N; 001 08.5E grid TR187684

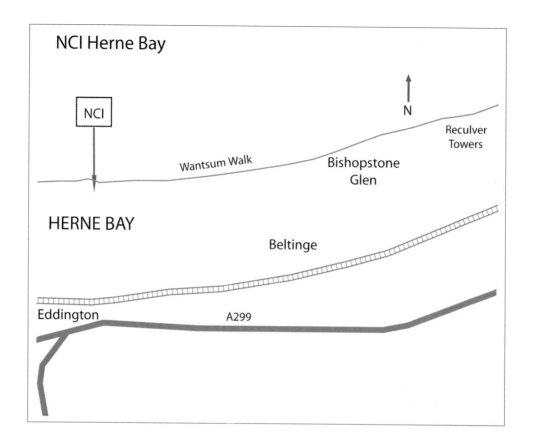

NCI Herne Bay

NCI

N

Reculver Towers

Wantsum Walk

Bishopstone Glen

HERNE BAY

Beltinge

Eddington

A299

The station is on the sea front and the lookout, 20ft above high water, gives a view along the north coast of Kent, from the remains of the church towers, the Reculver Towers (see colour section) to Warden Point on the Isle of Sheppey, covering a distance of fourteen miles. Here there are the remains of a concrete 'listening dish' – a precursor of radar.

The deepwater channels of the Thames Estuary are some ten miles offshore.

THE WATCH: TRAFFIC AND INCIDENTS

General craft monitored consist of pleasure craft, sailing dinghies, fishing boats and jet skis. In addition we monitor the shore and cliffs between Reculver and Neptune's Arm for walkers, bathers, and, during the summer, hang gliders launching from the cliff tops.

AND FINALLY...

Our watch station has been sold by the local council. The lease on the property expires in October 2010 but it is likely that the new owners will require us to vacate the premises before that date. We are now starting to look for suitable alternative sites.

Thames Region

NCI FELIXSTOWE

Station: NCI Lookout, Martello Tower, Wireless Green, Langer Rd, Felixstowe
Tel: 01394 670808
Station Manager: Keith Norgan, 589 Felixstowe Rd, Ipswich, IP3 8TE
Tel: 01473 725418
Email: ncifelixstowe@hotmail.co.uk
Website: www.coastwatch-online.org.uk
MCA Station: Thames
Declared Facility Status: 2006
Number of Volunteers: 31
Watch Hours: 09.00 – 17.00 (weekends and Bank Holidays)

HISTORY

Felixstowe NCI began its first watch in 1995 from a caravan which was towed each weekend into position for observations. From there it graduated to beach huts mounted on oil drums and concrete, premises which it shared with Alby's beach café and ice cream kiosk!

On 26 April 1998 the watch moved to its present home at the imposing Martello Tower (the name derives from the design of a fort at Mortella in Corsica) originally built along with a chain of others on the south coast to provide early warning of Napoleon's invasion – which did not take place – and later used by HM Coastguard. The wooden structure built on the roof of the tower gives a most advantageous view of the coast from 45ft.

LOCATION
51 56.5N; 001 20.1E grid TR293332

The station on the Suffolk coast sits between Felixstowe, the holiday resort, and Felixstowe, the largest containership port in the UK. Angled windows afford a wide view of the Harwich Approaches, again one of the busiest shipping areas in the UK, with a three-lane separation channel in operation for commercial traffic.

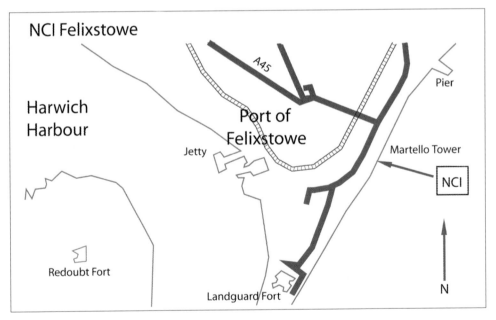

NCI Felixstowe

Harwich
Harbour

A45

Port of
Felixstowe

Jetty

Pier

Martello Tower

NCI

Redoubt Fort

Landguard Fort

N

THE WATCH: TRAFFIC AND INCIDENTS

With Felixstowe's dual functions as a port and a resort, the watch has to deal with a variety of traffic from logging the largest containerships in the world to a child adrift on an airbed. In addition the local rivers Orwell, Debden and Stour carry both trading and leisure craft. In 2005 thirty major incidents were logged by the station with Thames Coastguard. NCI Felixstowe has thus become a focal point of contact for the Beach Patrol, St John's Ambulance, coastguard and RNLI.

One major incident which, while not being beyond the call of normal duty, was none the less unusual, occurred on 25 September 2005 when the watch spotted a fire in a building known as the *Hermon DeStern*. A 999 call was made and the fire brigade was soon on the scene. The dramatic photograph (see colour section, picture E), taken by Jim Williamson, was used by the press, BBC and ITN.

NCI HOLEHAVEN

Station: Old Harbour Masters Office, Haven Rd, Canvey Island, Essex
Tel: 01268 696971
Station Secretary Paul Roberts, 28 Avondale Rd, South Benfleet, Essex
Tel: 01268 756553
Email: pauljeanette@strebor.mail1.co.uk
Website: www.nci.org.uk
MCA Station: Thames
Number of Volunteers: 25
Watch Hours: 08.00 - 16.00

HISTORY
Formerly a harbourmaster's office of the Port of London Authority, it was leased to the NCI and opened on 7 November 1999. Recently the PLA have appointed a Havenmaster, and he regularly joins the watchkeepers to update our river information. He hopes, soon, to have his patrol vessel moored to the jetty. Although a very industrial site, the variety of military and leisure craft, often from visiting nations, makes the busy log entries interesting reading. The station is now well equipped thanks to the volunteers' fund-raising efforts and donations from industries, BP, Shell, Tilbury Power Station and many more local businesses and organisations.

LOCATION
51 30.706N 000 33.126E grid TQ771823

The station overlooks the Sea Reach to the Mid-Blyth sector of the Thames, and is flanked by the Oikos Oil Terminal, CI Gas Terminal and BP Coryton.

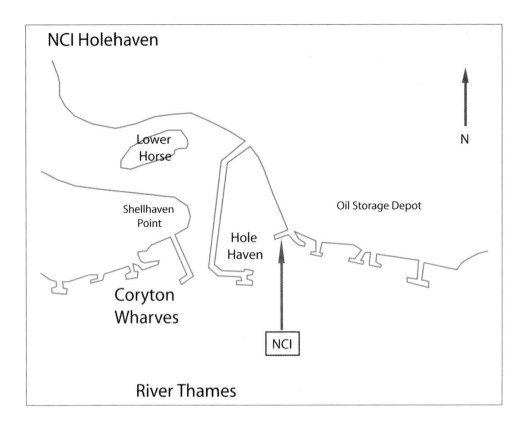

NCI Holehaven

Lower
Horse

Shellhaven
Point

Oil Storage Depot

Hole
Haven

NCI

Coryton
Wharves

River Thames

N

THE WATCH: TRAFFIC AND INCIDENTS

The station monitors all passing river traffic on a daily basis. This includes all manner of commercial vessels using the docks and jetties of the River Thames, a busy small fishing industry, as well as all types of leisure craft. The station keeps a watch on the many craft moored in the 'trot' of Holehaven. As a result of the latter, watchkeepers' records enabled the police to trace a stolen boat and apprehend the culprits. The watchkeepers were the first to report dolphin sightings in the Thames sea reaches, and maintained a sightings diary for local conservationist groups.

NCI SOUTHEND

Station: c/o QinetiQ, Sentinel House, Blackgate Rd, Shoeburyness, Essex, SS3 9SR
Tel (Mob.): 07815 945210
Email: general@ncisouthend.org.uk
Station Manager: Mike Taverner, 52 Waterford Rd, Shoeburyness, SS3 9HH
Tel: 01702 295446
Email: miketaverner@waterford52.freeserve.co.uk
MCA Station: Thames coastguard
Number of Volunteers: 10
Watch Hours: 09.00 – 17.00 (weekends)

HISTORY

NCI Southend, which opened in 1998, carried out its first watches from the premises of a local yacht club, and then from an empty first-aid post, before moving to a small caravan which was towed on and off site at Shoeburyness East Beach. In spring 2002 a plot of land was offered on the site of the old Shoebury garrison by Glade Dale Homes Ltd, and the station purchased two portakabins in which to house the watch. The watch in this location was officially opened by the Mayor of Southend on 11 August 2002. Unfortunately this location also proved temporary as, in December 2003, the station was given notice that its lease would not be renewed.

At this point the future for NCI Southend appeared bleak with very little practical help in the offing. However, Station Manager Michael Taverner wrote a second time to QinetiQ, managers for the MoD site at Shoeburyness, his request for a site there having been earlier refused. Thankfully QinetiQ *were* interested on this occasion, and the station was invited to set up their portakabins at Shoeburyness, on the site of the old Shoebury artillery range. The new station was opened on Easter Saturday 2004 and is now a thriving concern (five homes in as many years must be an NCI record!).

LOCATION

51 32.00N; 000 48.32E

grid TQ946853

NCI Southend has a position which provides visual coverage of the entire Thames estuary. On the north shore we can see from the old Mulberry harbour down to the Whittaker beacon at the mouth of the river. On the Kent shore we can see from the mouth of the Medway to Whitstable and onwards to the Reculver Towers. We can see the main anchorages for vessels waiting to go up the Medway or up to Tilbury. Further off the wind farm on the Kentish Flats, with thirty-two sails, is visible.

This beats the caravan!

THE WATCH: TRAFFIC AND INCIDENTS

The watch is a busy one and monitors all ships and yachts approaching and leaving the Thames and the Medway. Local beaches attract bathers, fishermen, windsurfers and horse riders, all of whom can be vulnerable to strong tides in the estuary. On 5 November 2005, with a SW Force 4 blowing, several wind surfers were taking advantage of the conditions. At the eastern end of the beach there is a boom which extends over a mile into deep water. One surfer was blown straight over the boom and out into the North Sea. He abandoned his kite and attempted to swim back to the boom against the tide. The watch alerted the coastguard and the lifeboat was tasked to pick up the survivor who was taken to Southend Hospital for observation.

South Coast Region

NCI NEWHAVEN

Station: Old Coastguard Lookout, Castle Hill, Newhaven
Tel: 01273 516464
Station Manager: Tony Fortnam, 3 Cobbe Pl, Beddigham, Lewes, BN8 6JY
Tel: 01273 858427
Email: tony.fortnam@btopenworld.com
Website: www.ncinewhaven.org.uk
MCA Station: Solent
Number of Volunteers: 42
Watch hours: 08.00 – 18.00

HISTORY

NCI Newhaven lookout is perched on the clifftop over 250ft above sea level. This provides a panoramic view over both Newhaven Harbour entrance and Seaford Bay. The seaward view gives an uninterrupted watch over 500 square miles of sea. The lookout is housed in the former coastguard lookout built in 1964 to replace a small lookout inside Newhaven Fort, a clifftop fort built in 1871, following a review of UK coastal defences commissioned by the then Prime Minister Lord Palmerston (the fort is now open to the public, details to be found at www.newhavenfort.org.uk). In 1974 six new coastguard houses and an office were built at Fort Road. This was the start of constant watch being kept at the lookout. It was manned by six full-time coastguards, supported by a dozen auxiliaries, who were also part of the cliff rescue team. The lookout's sturdy construction has stood the test of time including the battery of the 1987 hurricane, when it only lost a few windows.

In 1994, following the reorganisation of the coastguard service under the Maritime and Coastguard Agency (MCA), the lookout was no longer used for constant watch, though it continued to be used for casualties, working until 2002 when it was finally abandoned. With the support of local people, Newhaven Town Council and the Castle Hill Group (the local volunteer conservation group which looks after the nature reserve where the lookout is situated), Lewes District Council took over the building and leased it to the NCI in June 2004.

Newhaven lookout opened with about twenty-five volunteers, concentrating initially on weekend working. Since then there has been important and continuing support from local MP Norman Baker, Lewes District Council and the station's patron Viscount Hampden. The chair of East Sussex County Council confirmed the region's support for the NCI when she visited the lookout in October 2004. Cllr Bagshawe said, 'I was impressed by the professionalism and enthusiasm shown by the NCI volunteers. They fought hard and long to keep the Tower open when the MCA had planned to demolish it. Their work could literally mean the difference between life and death for someone in trouble.' On 1 January 2005 watches were extended to daily, and a year later the coverage was extended to 08.00 - 18.00 hrs, with a number of evening watches until 22.00 also maintained.

We have good working links with the Newhaven lifeboat, and recently joined them in an exercise.

LOCATION
50 46.95N 000 2.90E grid TQ 446001

The map shows the location of the lookout at the end of Fort Rise, off Fort Road, which runs along the west side of the port. For spectacular views of the changing weather, as seen from the watch, see colour section, pictures 24 and 25.

THE WATCH: TRAFFIC AND INCIDENTS
Commercial users of the Port of Newhaven include the car ferries to Dieppe (see colour section, picture 27), regular dredgers which unload shingle for the building trade, scrap metal carriers, the local fishing fleet and sea angling charter boats. There are also year-round surfers, hang gliders and divers operating offshore.

There are several local boatyards, a local marina and two sailing clubs. In summer the local beaches are busy with swimmers and inflatables. The station works closely with the local lifeboat station where a Severn-class lifeboat is on permanent standby. The logging of vessels varies with the seasons and the weather. An examination of the station log shows that there are roughly forty to fifty entries between 08.00 and 18.00 during a typical weekday in summer – but the 'small white motor boat with two p.o.vs.' threatens to monopolise any watchkeepers' attention during this period! In winter the average is about half that number.

In July 2005 the station picked up a call on Channel 16 from a yacht asking for assistance. There was no response from the coastguard. We then relayed the message to Solent Coastguard, confirming that the yacht was under our visual observation. The yacht was subsequently towed into harbour.

In September 2005 the watchkeeper spotted a day boat off the harbour near the main shipping channel with two p.o.vs. waving for help. He called the coastguard on 999 and the lifeboat subsequently towed in the casualty.

At 19.30 on an October evening in 2005 a red flare was spotted and the estimated position was reported to the coastguard. This resulted in the vessel in distress being safely towed in by a local fishing vessel, monitored throughout by the coastguard through landline connection to the lookout. Conversely, the station has been instrumental in helping to avoid unnecessary emergency

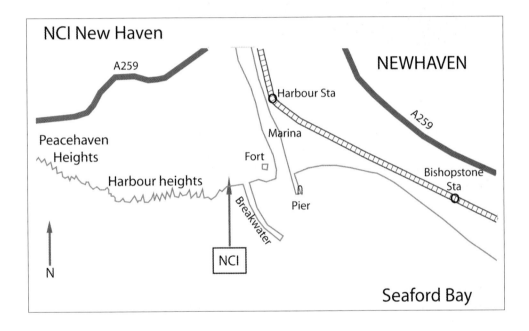

It's that swv 2pov again.

responses following 999 calls by members of the public when visual observation from the lookout has shown no cause for concern – when a log in the water is not 'an upturned boat'!

AND FINALLY…

The Greenwich Meridian is about three miles to the west of the lookout. This means that it is very easy for all concerned to make errors in reporting longitude positions – a factor which needs to be constantly borne in mind by watchkeepers. There has in fact been one incident where the station realised that a vessel had made such an error and was able to ensure that the lifeboat was redirected to the proper location.

NCI GOSPORT

Station: Signal Tower, Fort Blockhouse
MoD, Gosport, Hampshire, PO12 2RS
Tel: 02392 765194
Mob: 07503315539
Station Manager: Richard McMinn, 153 Albemarle Ave, Hardway, Gosport, PO14 4HT
Tel: 02392 588332
Email: richard_mcminn@hotmail.com
MCA Station: Solent
Watch Hours: 10.00 – 16.00 (weekends)

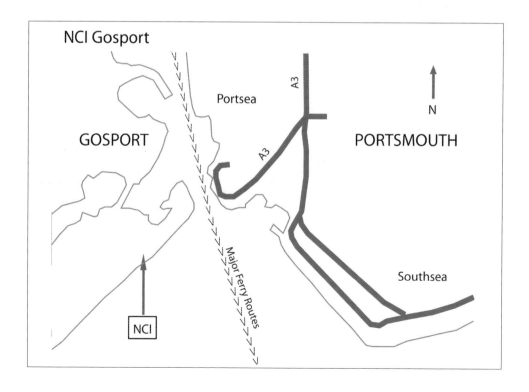

LOCATION
Lat: 50 47.38N Long: 001 6 72W OS: SZ 6268 9928

NCI SOLENT

Station: Beach Rd Car Park,
Marine Parade East, Lee on Solent, Hampshire,
　PO13 9LA
Tel: 02392556758
Manager: John Lee, Flat 34, Glamis Ct, Vicarage
　La, Stubbington, Fareham
Tel: 01329 661788
Email: lee1930@johnlee.force9.co.uk
MCA Station: Solent

LOCATION
Lat: 50 48N Long: 01 12W OS: SZ 5631 0045

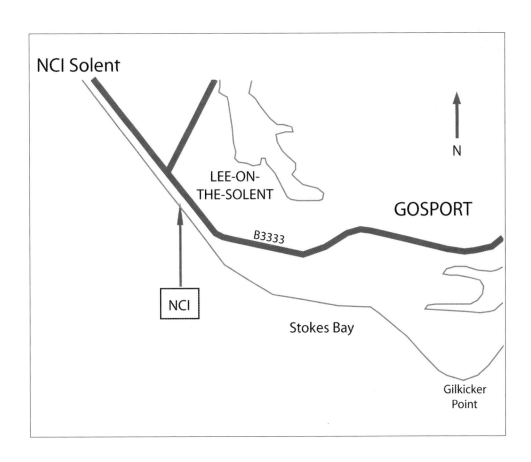

NCI SHOREHAM

Station: Old Fort Rd, Shoreham
Station Manager: Pauline Bradbury
Tel: 01273 516548
MCA Station: Solent
Watch Hours: 09.00 – 18.00   (Saturday and Sunday)

LOCATION
50.49,71 N 00 14 56 w grid os 104 523

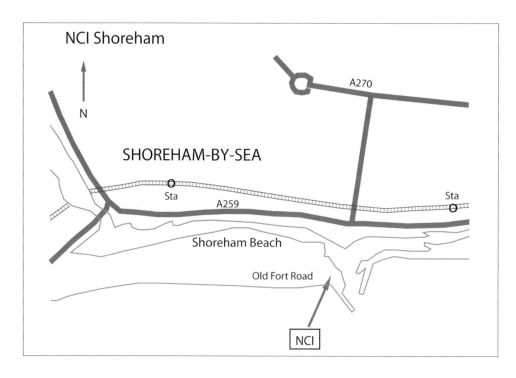

East Anglia Region

NCI GORLESTON

Station: NCI Lookout, South Pier, Gorleston, Great Yarmouth
Tel: 01493 440384
Station Manager: Jack Wells, 31 East Anglian Way, Gorleston, Norfolk, NR31 6TY
Tel: 01493 658424
Email: nurseryrhyme@uwclub.net
Website: www.coastwatch-online.org.uk/shorewatch/stations/Gorleston
MCA Station: Great Yarmouth
Declared Facility Status: 1996
Number of Volunteers: 50
Watch Hours: 08.00 - 20.00 (March to October), 08.00 - 19.00 (other months)

HISTORY

The NCI took over the first floor of the old Gorleston coastguard station in July 1994. The building is rented from the Great Yarmouth Port Authority, which retains port lights and other equipment on the roof and on the ground floor of the building.

We have the front watch room, an adjoining chart and book room, a storage room, a small kitchen with running water and a mains toilet.

Our watchkeepers have a wide range of experiences and past disciplines. These range from a retired vicar, electronic and radar engineers, hospital workers, retired teachers, an ex-captain of TH vessel *Patricia* and other local boat people with vast knowledge of our local sea and coastline.

THE LOCATION

52 34.33N 001 44.28 E grid TG534037

The lookout stands at the end of the South Pier at the entrance to Great Yarmouth Harbour at the mouth of the River Yare. The watch room is approx 10m above sea level. We have approximately sixty square miles visibility with a horizon of six and a half miles. To the south we look as far as Ness Point at Lowestoft and to the north Caister. From the side windows we can see Great Yarmouth beaches to Britannia Pier and Gorleston, Hopton beaches to the south.

THE WATCH: TRAFFIC AND INCIDENTS

The behaviour of the sea at the river mouth is extremely dangerous. The one hour time difference of tides at Beydon Water, three miles upriver, mixed with the tidal flow at sea, results in a sand bar at the harbour mouth together with a large crossflow of water in the mouth of the river. This phenomenon causes many small and sometimes large ships to get into trouble. There are sandbanks about a mile off, roughly parallel to the coast. There are two outlets through them for shipping, one via the Holm channel and the other north through Yarmouth Road. This means that vessels with a maximum draught of about 6m can enter the river and pass the station. Because the sands are constantly changing, surveys of this area are frequently made by the THV *Patricia*. Nineteen buoys mark this area for shipping. In summer Great Yarmouth is a busy holiday resort and has its share of jet skis, surfers and inflatables. Also the River Yare is the main outlet of sea-going motor cruisers that visit the Norfolk Broads, with many owners not fully experienced with the sea. All of these keep us on our toes. We have dealt with a variety of incidences from suicide attempts at the end of the pier to lost children.

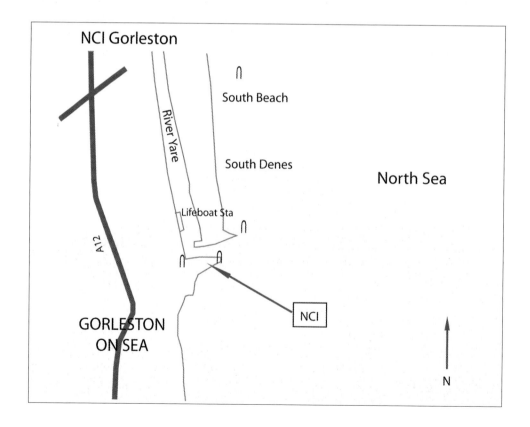

NCI WELLS-NEXT-THE-SEA

Station: Coast Guard Lookout, Pinewoods Holiday Park, Beach Rd, Wells-next-the-Sea
Tel: 01328 71058
Email: nciwells@tiscali.co.uk
Station Manager: (Chair) Dennis Woods, 47 Freeman St, Wells, NR11 8BG
Tel: 01328 711877
Email: denniswoods@onetel.com
MCA Station: Great Yarmouth
Number of Volunteers: 48
Watch Hours: 09.00 – 18.00 (summer) 09.00 – 16.00 (winter)

HISTORY

NCI Wells was opened on Easter Saturday 15 April 2006 on the site of the recently vacated coastguard lookout. The land is owned by the Earl of Holkham and a simple lease was negotiated between the NCI and Viscount Coke, the Earl's son. The lookout was constructed in 1970-71 and replaced the previous one situated a mile westward, which had begun to deteriorate after being inundated in the Great Flood of 1953. The new building was itself undermined during the floods of 1978, and was left standing on its brick plinth with the access stairway swept away. Happily the dune on which it stands is now protected by stoneworks.

HM Coastguard stopped using the lookout several years ago but maintained its lease because of the high aerial close to the west side of the building which was an important link in the coastguard radio network on the northern coast of Norfolk. The aerial, now used by the NCI, became redundant in July 2005 when a new radio tower was built at Langham, and the coastguard gave up its lease.

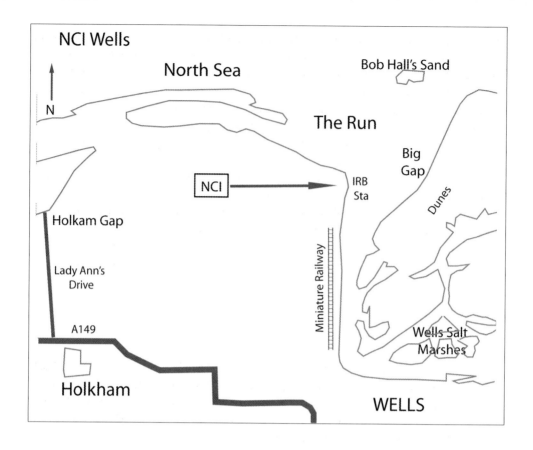

Wells-next-the-Sea, on the north Norfolk coast, has been a port and a largely natural safe haven for ships and boats for at least 600 years. Protected by rare salt marshes behind a sand bar, the Port of Wells was one of England's major harbours in Tudor times and a thriving centre for shipping and maritime industry in the nineteenth and early twentieth centuries, when its stone quay was constructed, along with many of the large buildings and tiny yards and houses that still dominate the look and feel of the town.

Commercial shipping in Wells suffered with the coming of the railway in 1857, but the harbour continued to be busy up to the First World War. There was something of a revival in the 1970s and '80s with ships of up to 300 tons regularly unloading on the quay. Indeed, commercial traffic arguably ended only in the late 1990s with cargoes of grain brought from Europe by the Dutch sailing ketch *Albatros* said, at the time, to be the last commercial trading vessel under sail in Europe.

However, Wells retains a fishing fleet of twelve vessels, with hard-working boats slipping out early on one tide and returning as soon as is practical on the next. They are joined on occasion by other visiting commercial and fishing vessels including, at the start of 2006, three survey vessels presently working on the docking shoals (see colour section, picture 30).

Wells Harbour now caters for a growing leisure trade, both for locally owned boats and, increasingly, as a popular destination for visiting vessels. The historic *Albatros* is currently resident on the quay, providing a venue for a variety of functions and entertainment and running the occasional charter or cruise. Another regular is the beautiful sailing barge *Juno*, built as a labour of love on a grand scale by local boatbuilder Charlie Ward, and now sailing day and half-day cruises. The high-speed RIB *Titan* offers coastal trips to see the seals at Blakeney. The harbour is also used for sailing, windsurfing, water-skiing and simply pottering about on anything from canoes and kayaks to speed boats, blue-water yachts and large motor cruisers (jet ski-type craft and hovercraft are not permitted). The town has a thriving sailing club, water-ski club and a successful new sailing school, offering plenty of opportunity for organised and entertaining activities for all ages and skill levels.

Situated in an area of outstanding natural beauty, Wells plays host to thousands of holidaymakers and visitors almost all year round, making for a unique mix of people and activities. The long tradition of gillying (fishing for shore crabs) from the quayside is as popular as ever, and Wells' expansive beach, with its oft-illustrated colourful beach-huts, means that there are always people on, in or near the water. It may not be the noisy maelstrom of 100 or 150 years ago but the quayside remains a busy, active place where it's fun to get involved or just to sit and watch all that's going on.

LOCATION
52 58.35N; 000 51.1E grid TF 915456

Wells NCI is located on the north Norfolk coast one mile north of the harbour, along Beach Road. It is situated on a sandy northern height, facing the buoyed channel into the harbour. It provides an ideal observation point overlooking Wells' beaches, Bob Hall Sands, and that part of the East Coast Shipping Route that passes through Race Channel. The Wells lifeboat station, with one offshore and one inshore boat, is 300 yards to the east.

THE WATCH: TRAFFIC AND INCIDENTS
The watch monitors all traffic in and out of the harbour. Today this consists mainly of yachts and pleasure craft.

The wide beaches are a great attraction for holidaymakers but they can often be traps for the unwary as the tide turns. To reach Bob Hall Sands some holidaymakers take the opportunity to cross 'The Run'. This becomes dangerous about two hours after low water when the flood tide begins to run at four to six knots.

RECENT SERVICES
7 October 2006, 09.02 a.m. A windsurfer was sailing in the harbour channel in blustery and difficult conditions on a strong ebbing tide. He lost his rig in the vicinity of Bob Hall Sands and was unable to retrieve it as it was swept out to sea by the outgoing tide. Wells coastwatch alerted Yarmouth coastguard to the situation. In the meantime the windsurfer managed to swim to the safety of the East Hills. At 09.02 the ILB was paged to render assistance. With the casualty in sight on the foreshore the ILB launched at 09.10 and was on scene by 09.18. The ILB returned to the lifeboat station with the casualty, where it was ascertained that he required no medical attention. Unfortunately the windsurfer's rig and board could not be located and the coastguard was notified of this. The ILB was re-fuelled and ready for service at 09.35. Wind: w6. Sea: Slight.

9 October 2006. The fishing vessel *Andora Star* was observed to lose a number of fishing trays while passing the Leading Buoy. Possible danger to small craft, monitored recovery.

The watch has also reported mooring buoys adrift, wild fowlers shooting in the vicinity of the beaches and three instances of dead seabirds to the state veterinary service. Since the autumn of 2006 we have, at the request of English Nature, kept an eye on a pod of seals which regularly come ashore in the vicinity of No.9 Buoy.

NCI MUNDESLEY

Station: The Watch House, Beach Rd, Mundesley, Norfolk, NR11 8BG
Tel: 01263 722399
Station Manager: Ray Ammo, 32 Warren Drive, Mundesley, NR11 8AS
Tel: 01263 721016
Email: nci.mundesley@googlemail.com
Website: www.nci.org.uk
MCA Station: Great Yarmouth
Number of volunteers: 50
Watch Hours: 08.00 – 18.00

HISTORY

The coastguard station at Mundesley was built in the early 1900s and was used as such until it was abandoned in the 1980s along with many other stations around the coast. In 1995 the building, owned by the Norfolk District Council, was leased to the NCI, and Mundesley Coastwatch came into being. The watch house is also home to the Mundesley Maritime Museum, on the top floor of which NCI has a lookout room.

LOCATION
52 52.68N; 001 26.3E
grid TG 315367

Coastwatch Mundesley

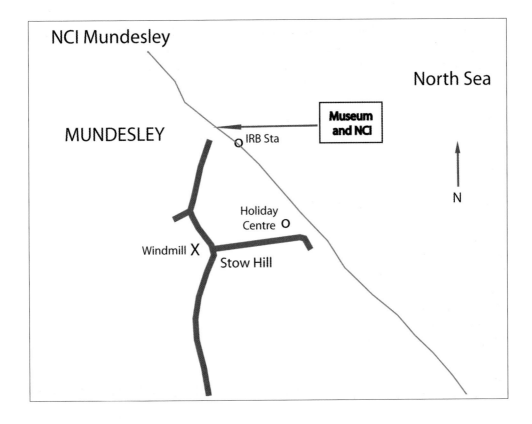

Situated on the sea front, the lookout has a clear view of sea traffic in the channels formed by the Haisborough sand bank nine miles parallel to the shore and the gas rigs approximately fourteen miles offshore. The nearest land opposite the lookout is the Island of Sylt at the border of Germany and Denmark giving us about 180 square miles of open sea viewing.

AND FINALLY...
One new landmark sited next to the lookout is the 'Mundesley Bomb'. This unexploded (defused) bomb was placed here to commemorate the lives of the REME bomb disposal team, killed while clearing mines from the Norfolk cliffs and beaches between 1944 and 1953. Twenty-six men died in this task, all between the ages of nineteen and thirty-nine (see colour section, picture 26).

North-West Region

NCI ROSSALL POINT (FLEETWOOD)

Station: The Promenade, Fleetwood, Lancashire
Tel: 01253 681378
Station Manager: Barry Ratner, 4 Chapel Close, Pilling, Lancs, PR3 6HF
Tel: 01253 790911
Email: barry.ratner@talktalk.net
MCA Station: Liverpool
Number of Volunteers: 28
Watch Hours: 10.00 - 18.00 (weekends and Bank Holidays)

HISTORY

Rossall Point sits on the south-west corner of the landmass comprising Morecambe Bay. The bay is treacherous, having a tidal range of 10m, and the land exposed at the ebb is almost exclusively sand which is always on the move, leaving banks that rise above 2m in places. The gullies, which intersect the banks, quickly fill as the tide returns, frequently cutting off the unwary. Most tragically, this was witnessed in the recent deaths of the Chinese cockle pickers.

The station was built for the coastguard in 1948 as one of a ring of watches around the bay. Abandoned by HM Coastguard in the 1990s, it has been a lookout for birdwatchers and a storage space for the local authority's gardeners. In 2007 the NCI approached Wyre Borough Council with a view to leasing it and after much debate and delay, which caused the loss of some potential members,

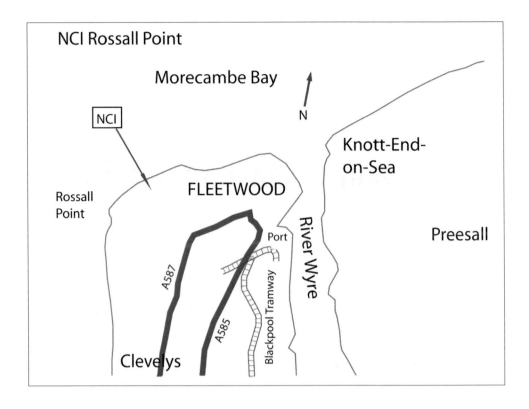

the NCI acquired possession in spring 2008. With the help of Fleetwood Nautical College and the voluntary efforts of lecturer Tom Jowett, lessons on chartwork were begun and the NCI training modules were adapted.

The station now has twenty-eight volunteers who man the station, mainly on weekends. While we monitor all traffic in the bay from commercial vessels to kite surfers and jet skis, as you can imagine our incident log chiefly concerns people stranded on the beaches during incoming tide. However, from our first watch we were called on by the Lancashire Police to guard a potential 'crime scene' – a flying suit which was thought to contain human remains. This, thankfully, was not the case.

LOCATION
53 55.38N 003 02.69W SD 120664

East and North-East Region

NCI HARTLEPOOL

Station: NCI Hartlepool Coastwatch, Ferry Rd, Middleton, Hartlepool, TS24 0SF
Tel: 01429 274931
Email: coastwatch@btconnect.com
Station Manager: (Chair) Doug Howe, 197 Kingsway Dve, Hartlepool, TS24 9SA
Tel: 01429 270670
Website: Under development
MCA Station: Humber coastguard (Bridlington)
Declared Facility Status: May 2002, re-awarded August 2006
Number of Volunteers: 26
Watch Hours: Seven days each week, 08.00 - 16.00 hrs, but extended during school holidays and summer period. Hours are also extended on request from MCA

HISTORY

NCI Hartlepool was founded on 14 March 1997. The premises were formerly an old yacht club left empty and vandalised for some time. The building and surrounding land was given to the NCI by the Teesside Development Corporation. The founding members completely refurbished the building at their own expense, including everything from the kitchen sinks and toilet bowls to cleaning and decorating, as well as equipping the bridge. Hartlepool Coastwatch remains indebted to those volunteers and the assistance given by local firms. Today the building boasts an excellent weatherproof watch deck above a social facility that includes training and storage rooms, a dance floor and licensed bar.

LOCATION

54 41.6N; 001 11.4W grid NZ 523335

Hartlepool Coastwatch overlooks Hartlepool Bay, standing about 15m above the nearby beach (Middleton Strand). It and the adjacent RNLI lifeboat station are accessible by road from the town centre.

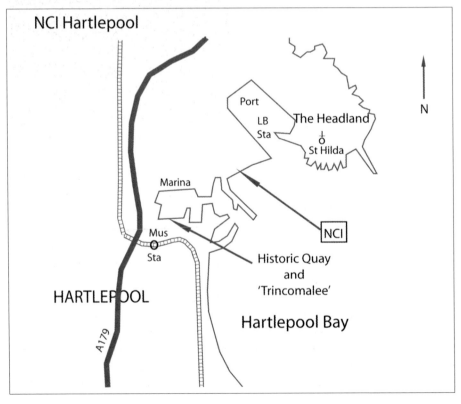

NCI Hartlepool

THE WATCH: TRAFFIC AND INCIDENTS

Within 80m of our east windows (to our left) is the dredged channel leading to Hartlepool Harbour. From these windows we have a clear view across the channel to the well-used public beach, Fish Sands, which is backed by the fourteenth-century town wall. To the south-east is the Heugh Breakwater (see colour section, picture 7), which, whilst often overwashed by the North Sea, is the haunt of many rod fishermen.

Traffic passing these windows is typically offshore and inshore fishing vessels but may include 50,000-ton deep sea cargo vessels, newly built oilrig components or juveniles on a lilo (see colour section, picture 31).

To the right of our south windows is the entrance to Hartlepool Marina, currently the home of around 400 vessels. These range from working survey and fishing boats through all types of leisure craft, including a couple of narrow boats. West of the marina, public beaches curve for some three miles due south to the mouth of the Tees. The controlled traffic from this major commercial port follows a buoyed channel running north-east/south-west some three miles from our windows. Beyond the Tees the beaches swing southeast to Redcar and the 100m-high cliffs near Saltburn. These cliffs are lost to view near Whitby, about seventeen miles from Hartlepool Coastwatch.

Traffic from these windows may be summarised by the general observation logged by a watchkeeper one summer's day morning: 'There are currently twenty-nine moving vessels in sight.' Vessels recorded included deep sea bulkers and tankers moving to and from anchorages off Hartlepool and Redcar, or the controlled Tees Channel, and commercial onshore and offshore fishing boats. Commercial and private rod fishing boats and a smattering of leisure motorboats and sailboats complete the scene. Additionally, at weekends we see regattas and races by the local yacht club. Occasionally there are some near misses. This windsurfer cuts it fine!

An example of a non-routine incident illustrates the wider value of the NCI in this community. In the summer of 2003 a small inland thunderstorm rapidly developed vigour over north Teesside. In Hartlepool the summer morning darkened until the streetlights came back on and wind drove rain almost horizontally into flooding streets. In the Tees Bay sixteen individual Mayday calls were registered around midday. Sterling service was given by the RNLI around the bay. The duty observer at Hartlepool was able to direct a returning lifeboat to a swimmer marooned on a channel buoy. As the storm moved away observers at Hartlepool (with the aid of local knowledge) were able to advise the many concerned relatives of boating folk who rang or visited the station. More formally, a three-hour-long liaison with the coastguard ensued to establish the safe whereabouts of vessels recorded as departing Hartlepool that morning. Some had run for sea room and others had swung to shelter inshore. Regrettably, a fatality resulted from the one boat that was destroyed. Around midday observers recalled seeing the anemometer gauge needle falling towards Force 9. Weather reports logged at 10.00 and 14.00 hrs recorded pleasant sunny weather – such was the speed of passage of the storm.

Hartlepool Coastwatch participates in the Cleveland Emergency Joint Planning Committee, the East Coast Sea Defences Group and a local project to preserve the Victoria breakwater, the Heugh. Uniformed members attend the Remembrance Sunday parade. This year a member placed the merchant navy wreath. After the ceremony numbers of civic and military guests meet in the watch for a buffet lunch with members and friends. Similarly, after the ceremony of the Blessing of the Sea guests remain for a buffet.

Hartlepool Marine Festival (see colour section, picture 33) attracts between 10-20,000 spectators to the marina. Uniformed members patrol the marina with radio links to a safety control, to provide eyes for the safety boats. Some vessels of the Tall Ships visited the marina and the deep water port in 2005. Hartlepool Coastwatch has been booked as the control centre by the organisers of the visit in 2010 of the Tall Ships.

AND FINALLY...

Harry Carter, almost a founding member, who clocked up 1,500 hours of watchkeeping by doing the 8-10.00 'early watch' for three years, received a personal commendation from the Mayor of Hartlepool. Harry continued watching until overcome by illness. Hartlepool Coastwatch was pleased to carry his ashes and those of another member to a grassy slope facing the sea, where they are warmed by the morning sun.

SUNDERLAND VOLUNTEER LIFE BRIGADE (SVLB) COASTWATCH
(AFFILIATED TO NCI)

Station: Roker Watch House, Pier View
Tel: 01915 672579
Senior watch Officer: Fred Roberts
Secretary: Mrs R. Roberts, 61 Farrow
    Drive, Whitburn, Sunderland, SR6 7BQ
Tel: 01915 292651
Email: roberts61@btinternet.com
Website: www.sunderlandvlb.com
MCA Station: Humber MRSC
Declared Facility Status: 2007
Number of Volunteers: 16
Watch Hours: 10.00 - 16.00 (weekends)

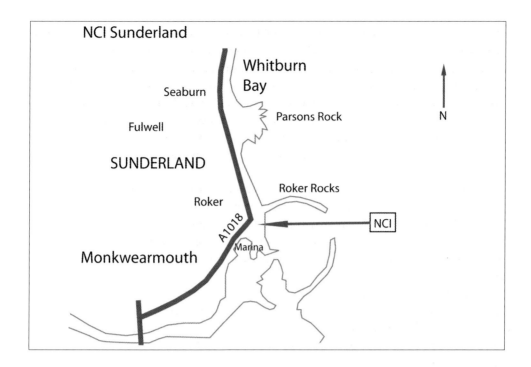

HISTORY

Sunderland Coastwatch opened on 15 October 2005 as part of the Sunderland Volunteer Life Brigade, which was founded in 1877 to do ship-to-shore rescue by Breeches Buoy. The SVLB saved more than 800 lives here, including a record 272 men from two stranded destroyers in 1940. Team members at this time were auxiliary coastguards. Breeches Buoy became obsolete in 1983, at which time the SVLB became a 'Declared Facility' coastal search and cliff rescue team, available twenty-four hours each day, 365 days a year.

After assessment in March 2007 the Coastwatch was added to the existing 'Declared Facility' coastwatch status. As more members are recruited and trained the coastwatch will operate seven days a week. Sunderland Coastwatch is unique because it is the only coastwatch team which is part of an organisation, which also has a coastal search and cliff rescue team.

In 2007 the SVLB celebrated the 130th anniversary of its founding. The station for both services is Roker Watch House, built in 1906. The watch house is also home to a museum featuring the wreck and rescue data of the last 130 years. The watch house will become an accredited museum in the future. It will then be the nearest thing to a maritime museum in Sunderland. Like the NCI, the SVLB is independent of the coastguard and is a charitable organisation.

LOCATION

54 55.27N; 001 21.92W grid NZ 408587

The watch house is situated overlooking the Sunderland Harbour entrance. The harbour has Roker Pier to the north and the South Pier to the south. At the end of Roker Pier stands Roker lighthouse.

THE WATCH: TRAFFIC AND INCIDENTS

All inward and outward traffic is logged to include craft description and number of persons onboard. Traffic includes coastal commercial ships, local fishing craft, sail and motor pleasure craft. Most yachts tend to do summer sailing only. Weather reports are sent to Humber MRSC at the beginning and end of the watch. A descriptive spreadsheet and photographic record is updated as new craft are identified and maintained on the lookout computer. This has become invaluable in identifying craft that have been involved in incidents requiring assistance from either the Sunderland lifeboats and/or Humber MRSC.

Sunderland crest.

On 1 October 2006, Sunderland Coastwatch assisted the coastguard and lifeboat service in identifying a boat which had been reported to be on fire off Beacon Hill, Easington. The Sunderland lifeboat contacted a vessel in the immediate vicinity of the sighting and obtained the name and description of a fishing boat which had left the area after having had an engine fire. SVLB duty coastwatchers recognised the name and description from the log as that of a fishing boat which had since returned to Sunderland Harbour. SVLB coastwatch advised Humber MRSC of this information and the lifeboat was able to ascertain that the vessel was safe in Sunderland Harbour. Paul Nicholson, senior helmsman of Sunderland RNLI, praised the SVLB coastwatch as a vital link in the chain during the incident.

NCI SKEGNESS

Station: Old Cog Station, Winthorpe Avenue, Skegness, Lincolnshire, PE25 1QY
Tel: 01754 610900
Email: nciskegness@aol.com
Station Manager: Mike Newbold, Sawubona, Vicarage Lane, Wainfleet, St Mary, Skegness, PE24 4JJ
Tel: 01754 880960 **Mobile:** 07831 220299
Deputy Station Manager: Roger Gilburd, Cygnus, 17 Washdyke Lane, Mumby, Alford,
Lincolnshire, LN13 9JY
Tel: 01507 490878
Mobile: 07810 264778
MCA Station: Humber MRSC
Declared Facility Status: February 2007
Number of Volunteers: 30
Watch Hours: BST: 09.00 – 18.00
GMT: 09.00 – dusk

HISTORY

In March 2004 a ten-year lease was taken on the old lifeguard station at Ingoldmells Point near Skegness in Lincolnshire, being leased from the then owners Laver Leisure. This was refurbished, re-decorated and re-opened.

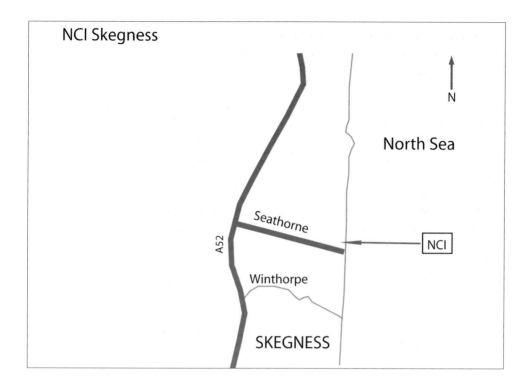

NCI Skegness

North Sea

N

Seathorne

A52

NCI

Winthorpe

SKEGNESS

Since then the station was operational seven days a week throughout the year, being attributed and credited with saving no less than twenty-three lives, possibly more.

2005 saw a completely new team at Ingoldmells Point, which rapidly grew to twenty-five highly trained watchkeepers. Alas, in the early days the Ingoldmells coastwatch tower attracted the unwelcome attention of local vandals, and continued countermeasures took place, including roll down security shutters and other security measures, all costing money which could have been better spent on safety equipment.

Following much fund-raising activities, the old station was upgraded with the installation of marine VHF radios on the emergency channels, long-distance radar, new high-power binoculars, automatic ship identification and computers.

Since it commenced regular operations in March 2005, the NCI coastwatch station at Ingoldmells Point has kept a visual safety observation on the three miles of shoreline, beach and promenade between Chapel Point and Butlin's foreshore. In June 2008, however, the Ingoldmells Point beach owners requested NCI to cease operations as the building was apparently 'in imminent danger of collapse' – hence, NCI Ingoldmells Point was no more. Recognising the value of the NCI service and their plight, East Lindsey District Council immediately granted a lease on the old coastguard tower at Winthorpe Road, Seathorne, near Skegness. This new location was refitted, re-wired, re-decorated, re-rigged and operational with ten days. NCI Skegness recommenced operations on a year round, seven days a week basis.

LOCATION
Lat: 53 09.983N Long: 000 21.056E OS: TF 5722 6419

Resolution.

LOOKING SOUTH TOWARDS SKEGNESS
Our new panorama is from one mile north, at Whitehouse Corner, to three miles south to Skegness' south beach – a very busy surveillance area which includes much commercial holiday traffic and commercial fishing activity. Across the wash, we can normally observe Norfolk coastline at some thirteen miles distance, and all the shipping going to and from the ports of Boston and Sutton Bridge. Close by we have both Wainfleet and Donna Nook military bombing ranges, so a lot of aircraft activity.

Also in our domain are the new Lynn and inner Dowsing wind farms currently under construction by Centrica Renewables (a division of British Gas). Due to the commanding position of the NCI Skegness coastwatch tower, the construction company have asked NCI Skegness to host their remote private marine VHF communications channel and base station for the three-year duration of the build.

The picture above shows *Resolution*, a six–leg jacked-up heavy-lift construction vessel, now semi-resident two miles east of our tower, sustained by a plethora of support, survey and safety vessels, including an accommodation ship.

THE WATCH: TRAFFIC AND INCIDENTS
Incidents dealt with include inflatables being blown out to sea with children on them, lost and found children, dangerous munitions, sinking vessels, lost vessels, surfboarders in distress, swimmers exhausted, seals and pups rescued, large debris removed, chemical containers, fires, crime, carcases, attempted suicides and many more.

Thankfully, close by in Skegness we have the RNLI lifeboats with a Mersey-class all-weather lifeboat *Lincolnshire Poacher*, and a D-class ILB *Leicester Fox II*, which are often called upon, as well as a new D-class RNLI inshore lifeboat, *William Hadley*, at Mabelthorpe, and resident HMCG mobile teams at Skegness, Chapel St Leonard's and Mablethorpe.

NCI MABLETHORPE

Station: The Chalet, Promenade, Mablethorpe
Station Manager: Bill Watson
Tel: 01507 472037
Website: nci.org.uk
MCA Station: Humber

Mablethorpe NCI is the most recent station to be opened on the east coast. The East Lindsey District Council has rented out a beach chalet on the promenade for the start up. Twenty-five volunteers have applied for training, which is being given by the Mablethorpe Coastguard and NCI trustee Mike Newbold and his lads from NCI 'Skeggy'.

South Wales Region

BARRY ISLAND (NELL'S POINT)

Station: Nell's Point, Barry Island, Vale of Glamorgan
Tel: 01446 420746
Email: nellspt@tiscali.co.uk
Station Manager: Clive Wilton
Tel: 01446 710374
Website: www.nci-nellspoint.org.uk
MCA Station: Swansea
Declared Facility Status: March 2009
Watch Hours: 08.00 – 17.00 (summer) 08.00 – dusk (winter)

LOCATION
51.23.24N 003. 15. 82w Grid ss 120664

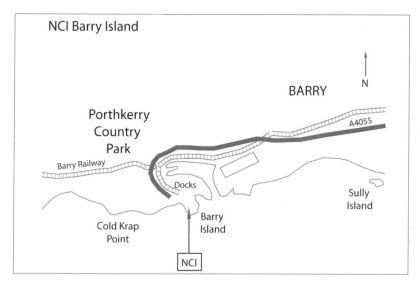

HISTORY

Work is now completed on a major refurbishment project at the former coastguard station at Nells Point, Barry Island. The Vale of Glamorgan Council is developing the building with funding from the Welsh Assembly's physical regeneration fund, and the project will complete works to restore the headland and improve public access.

The council is working in partnership with the NCI who have occupied the first floor of the building as the watch. Another key partner is Associated British Ports who operate a radar installation at the station to provide information on shipping using this busy part of the Bristol Channel.

WORMS HEAD

Station: The Old CG Station, Rhossili, Gower, South Wales
Tel: 01792 390167
Station Manager: Alan Richard
Tel: 01792 390497
MCA Station: Swansea
Declared Facility Status: March 2009
Watch Hours: 10.00–18.00 (summer) 10.00–16.00 (winter)

LOCATION

51 33.48N; 004 18.18W grid SS403875

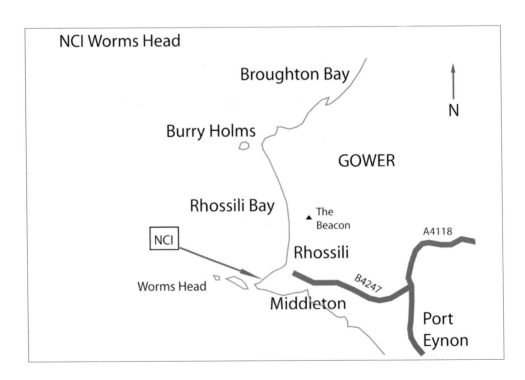

Stations Under Negotiation

JAYWICK (ESSEX)

ST MARY'S (SCILLY ISLANDS)

WHITBY

WOOLTACK POINT (MILFORD HAVEN)

WALNEY ISLAND (BARROW IN FURNESS)

FORT PERCH ROCK (NEW BRIGHTON)

PORT DINLLAEN (LLEYN PENNINSULA)

BRACH Y PWLL (LLEYN PENNINSULA)

PWLLHELLI

TORBAY

RHOSCOLIN (ANGLESEY)

WORKINGTON

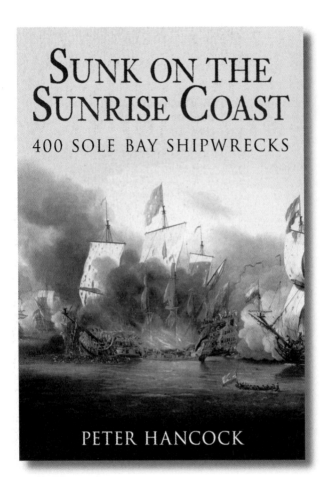

SUNK ON THE SUNRISE COAST: 400 SOLE BAY SHIPWRECKS

PETER HANCOCK

ISBN: 978 0 7524 4747 6

This fascinating book details the vessels that came into a bay on the Suffolk coast and never left it: sunk or stranded for the most part by gales, greed or gunshot; a timeworn minority abandoned or broken up where they lay. This work features information about the character of Sole Bay and the vessels that sailed its waters.

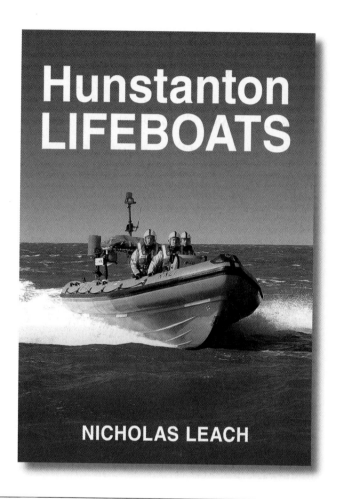

HUNSTANTON LIFEBOATS

NICHOLAS LEACH

ISBN: 978 0 7524 4749 0

This comprehensive work trace the story of Hunstanton's lifeboat station from its origins in the nineteenth century through to the present day, detailing all of its launches, rescues and key personnel. The book includes a sixteen-page colour picture section which takes the reader to the heart of the action and reveals in new detail the vital work of the lifeboats in saving lives along this stretch of Norfolk's north–west coast.

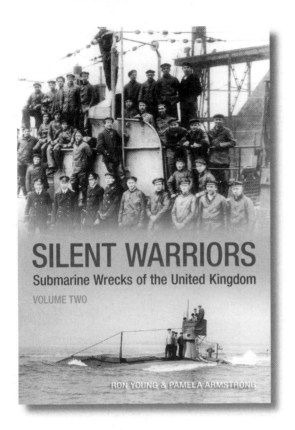

SILENT WARRIORS
Submarine Wrecks of the United Kingdom
VOLUME TWO

RON YOUNG & PAMELA ARMSTRONG

Silent Warriors: Submarine Wrecks of the United Kingdom:

Vol. Two

Ron Young & Pamela Armstrong

ISBN: 978 0 7524 4789 6

Volume two of Ron Young and Pamela Armstrong's informative trilogy on submarine wrecks of the British Isles, focusing in this edition on the South Coast, from Beachey Head in Sussex down to the Isles of Scilly. Over 150 British submarine and U-boat wrecks in British coastal waters, specifically those in the English Channel, are described in detail, including information on the vessel's type and technical specifications, its voyage history, how it was sunk, a list of crew at the time of loss, details of the wreck site and the current state of the wreck.

The History Press